I WILL STAND & NOT BE MOVED

SPIRITUAL WARFARE FOR KIDS

A guide to teach & equip our children on how to be warriors in God's Army!

Jolene McCall

Spiritual Warfare for Kids
Copyright © 2015 by Hori-Son Press

All rights reserved. No portion of this book may be reproduced, stored in a retrieval system, or transmitted in any form or by any means electronic, mechanical photocopy, recording, or any other except for brief quotations in printed reviews, without the prior permission of the Publisher or Copyright Owner.

Printed in the United States of America

Cover Art by Lynn H. Pellerin

Lyrics to Song by Karmin M. Jones

ISBN 978-1-938186-02-8

SAN 920-251X

Throughout this book, the name satan has deliberately not been capitalized. To capitalize a name would be proper grammar, and it also shows respect to that person. Since, I have no respect for satan or any demonic force of that nature, I choose to be grammatically incorrect and refrain from capitalizing his name.

Scripture taken from the HOLY BIBLE, NEW INTERNATIONAL VERSION®. Copyright © 1973, 1978, 1984 Biblica. Used by permission of Zondervan. All rights reserved.

"Scripture taken from the New King James Version. Copyright © 1982 by Thomas Nelson, Inc. Used by permission. All rights reserved."

Scripture quotations marked NLT are taken from the Holy Bible, New Living Translation, copyright 1996, 2004. Used by permission of Tyndale House Publishers, Inc., Wheaton, Illinois 60189. All rights reserved.

"Scripture quotations taken from the Amplified® Bible, Copyright © 1954, 1958, 1962, 1964, 1965, 1987 by The Lockman Foundation. Used by permission." (www.Lockman.org)

"Scripture quotations marked (ESV) are from The Holy Bible, English Standard Version® (ESV®), copyright © 2001 by Crossway, a publishing ministry of Good News Publishers. Used by permission. All rights reserved."

Scripture quotations marked NLV are taken from the New Life Version copyright © 1969 and 2003. Used by permission of Barbour Publishing, Inc., Uhrichsville, Ohio, 44683. All rights reserved.

Scripture quotations marked HCSB®, are taken from the Holman Christian Standard Bible®, Copyright © 1999, 2000, 2002, 2003, 2009 by Holman Bible Publishers. Used by permission. HCSB® is a federally registered trademark of Holman Bible Publishers.

Public domain Bibles may be used freely, without restriction and without prior permission. The following Bibles in the English section of BibleGateway.com are in the public domain and can be used freely without restriction or prior permission from us or anyone else:

King James Version (Crown copyright/Public Domain in the United States)
American Standard Version (No copyright information is available)

Acknowledgements

A special thank you to my Father in Heaven as always! Without You Lord, I am nothing, but with You, I can do all things. I pray that the lessons within this book bring glory to You, alone. Every single day that I wake up and take that first breath is a blessing once again to be able to live and breathe in this world in which you have placed me. I thank you for the revelation as I seek you and for the opportunity to be able to touch lives through Jesus Christ knowing that through You lives are transformed. My words alone mean nothing if my actions are not one with You. I pray that You keep me close as I travel through the pathways of life. Lead me not into temptation Lord but deliver me daily as only You can do. Let my life be used for Your purposes and Your will always be done as I daily lay my life and my desires at the Cross with Jesus Christ.

I will stand and not be moved
I will stand Lord because of You
Where You lead me, I will go
Trusting You, the One I know

Through my trials and through the storms
Impacting lives for your return
Holding on until the end
I will trust Lord, where you send

I will stand and not be moved
Because of my great love for You
Through the thick and through the thin
Lord, knowing in the end we win

To my dearest grandchildren,

Jerrika

To my high-spirited grandchild,

I pray that nothing will ever prevent you from accomplishing all that Our Lord has placed on your heart. You are such a blessing as I watch your desires unfold and your talents manifest. Your great love for horses is amazing as I watch you ride without any cares on one of the most magnificent creatures in our world. As God prepares you in this life for the second coming of Jesus Christ, in all His magnificence, remember, Jesus will return with His army riding on a white horse. It is evident that God also loves horses and put that desire within you. Our time on this earth is all about drawing close to Our Father and that can be done in many ways. We seek Him, but we also find Him through all of His wonderful creations. Jesus said while praying one day to His Father, "They fail to recognize You..."

John 17:25 (AMP) [25] O just and righteous Father, <u>although the world has not known You and has failed to recognize You and has never acknowledged You</u>, I have known You [continually]; and these men understand and know that You have sent Me.

This world has failed to see Him because the enemy has placed so many obstacles in the way where they fail to "smell the roses" so to speak. In taking time out, we can all learn from an 8 year old little girl. God is in that horse. He is in the flowers and the trees. We can see Him in the clouds and in the rain. He is in the oceans and the seas. All of His creation is made for us to take time out to "pause" and reflect on just how great Our God is because He is all around us! Jerrika, be that light in a world of darkness as you take time out to "pause" and reflect on all the goodness of Our Lord Jesus Christ. I love you very much!

~

Charli

To my little oak tree,

There was a saying by an unknown poet, "The mighty oak was once a little nut that stood its ground." As I read that saying, I thought of you. You are my little nut, dynamite in a small package. As I watch you interact with this world, growing and learning, I learn from you. Even though you may be small, deep within your little spirit grows a mighty oak. We are all created in different packaging but what is on the inside determines our destiny in this life. Your little size means absolutely nothing to you as you step out independently ready to conquer this ever changing world. I watch you from a distance as you interact with others and step forth to challenges beyond a 3-year old capacity; however, the determination within you keeps you treading forward and never retreating. You have a fighter mentality within that says, "I will not give up and I will not quit!" It is this strength within that will carry you far in this life. As that small seed within you continues to grow in beauty and strength, just like the mighty oak, always remember your roots. The mighty oak possesses all of its strength from deep within its root system. Your roots carry you all the way back to your Creator just like that of the oak. God has placed within you all that you are made of, and He will see you through every single storm in this life. Though the storms come and go, the mighty oak will sway back and forth. Many limbs may be weakened which fall or are removed, but the oak remains standing as long as it is rooted deep within healthy soil. You too will face many storms in this life and these storms will remove from you those things that weaken you. Allow the trials in this life; remain connected to that which is healthy, and let go of those areas which will weaken you and bring you down.

Isaiah 61:3 (NLT) ³To all who mourn in Israel, he will give a crown of beauty for ashes, a joyous blessing instead of mourning, festive praise instead of despair. In their righteousness, they will be like great oaks that the LORD has planted for his own glory.

It is evident to see that God has given you a strong-will, but with that strong-will, you will have to endure many tests in this life in order that He molds you in the image of Jesus Christ. Remain righteous in the sight of the Lord always, and He will create within you a perfect heart! Love you my baby!

~

Silas

To my first grandson,

I never had a son of my own and wasn't sure that I would have even known how to raise a boy. My closest experience to being around little boys was witnessing how they were always dirty, bullying little girls, and constantly being reprimanded by their parents for misbehaving. I remember being thankful that I never had the task of raising a boy myself. However, watching you grow has definitely given me a different insight into the delight of having a son or rather, a grandson. Yes, you are still that little boy that dirt seems to attach to even when you never go outside. Your mother one day was telling me that she just didn't understand where the dirt came from. My response was that boys were made from the dust of the ground while girls were made from their rib; therefore, maybe the dirt did come from the inside until it reached the outside of little boys. I hope that someday this will bring you a big smile from your Gammy, but I want you to know that inside of you is a very gentle spirit. I see a boy that is gentle and quiet, one that will listen intently and obey when told. You, Silas, have that protective spirit when it comes to others and a love that flows out to those you are close to. All of your names – Daniel – Elijah – Silas are those of a prophet. Our family has been blessed with prophesy, and God is preparing you for something spectacular. I know through experience that sometimes it seems that God is not moving fast enough, but God is seldom early and He is never ever late. Trust in the Lord your God with all your heart and lean not to your own understanding. In all you do, Silas, trust in Him and He will see you through. Expect the impossible and hold fast to those dreams and visions that will be given to you by your Father in Heaven.

I love you very much and see a great man of God in the makings. Forgive always those that mistreat you and pray for your enemies while experiencing a move of God that will be phenomenal as you trust. Love you!

~

Josiah

To my second grand-son,

You are only 1 year old and your personality is just barely beginning to manifest. I can say that you are small in size, but you remind me of the little Chihuahua puppy daring the Great Dane to take their food. Watching you interact with your brother, who is about 3 times your size, is amazing. When he upsets you, you continue to walk to where he is while trying to hurt him physically. You are not able to hurt him because of your size, but you think that you can! It is amazing what must go through your mind. Your mother has to actually get on to you for trying to hurt him. God definitely has plans for you but of course, there will be that time of preparation where you will be tested and humbled. Your name Josiah in Hebrew means the fire of the Lord or the Lord burns. In the bible, Josiah became King of Judah at only 8 years old. During his rule, he set out to cleanse the land from idolatry by destroying altars and images of pagan deities and bringing the Ark of the Covenant to the Temple.

In addition to your first name, your second name has quite a remarkable meaning, William. William was derived from a German name Willhelm. There are two meanings – one is "will or desire" and the other is "helmet or protection." William became very popular after the Norman Conquest of England lead by the first Norman King of England and usually known as William the Conqueror. I see two things that God has placed within you, but to carry this through, your steps must follow in the path of Our Creator, Jesus Christ. First, your will or desires must be joined with God the Father. As you begin your journey into adolescence and onto adulthood, be careful in following your heart unless it has been broken and humbled by Our Lord. Your helmet must be on daily as you will be one to offer protection and truth to those that look up to you but only if you have gained your knowledge through the Word of God. His desire – not your desire and you will go far in the Kingdom of Heaven bringing great wisdom to the saints. Be strong and courageous my dear grand-son, for much will be given to you but not to be stored, only to give away. Take heart knowing that prayers have gone out for you to prepare you for your calling. Seek Him first and all things will be added to your days. I love you dearly!

~

Table of Contents

Acknowledgement... iii

Introduction... 1

Outline of Class SWKBI.. 23

Outline of Class SWKBII....................................... 25

Parent's Guide/Song... 27

Example Prayer for Armor.................................... 31

Spiritual Warfare for Kids Beginners I

    Lesson 1... 37

    Parent's Review... 41

    Lesson 2... 67

    Parent's Review... 71

    Lesson 3... 85

    Parent's Review... 89

    Lesson 4... 105

    Parent's Review... 109

Spiritual Warfare for Kids Beginners II

- Lesson 1 119
- Lesson 2 121
- Parent's Review 123
- Lesson 3 139
- Parent's Review 141
- Lesson 4 153
- Parent's Review 155

Conclusion by Author 183

References 184

Introduction

Spiritual Warfare for Kids Beginners I and Beginners II

Designed for Teachers and Parents

As Christians, we need to understand how important it is to recognize the spiritual realm. The spiritual realm is very real even though we may not be able to see it with our natural eyes. However, just as we believe there is a God and that Jesus is very much alive today, even though we cannot see them, there is also a realm that is invisible in the natural. In this realm, the Holy Spirit was sent to be our Comforter. We cannot see the Holy Spirit, but it is through Him that we are taught all things and reminded of all truths.

John 14:25-26 (NKJV) [25] "These things I have spoken to you while being present with you. [26] But the Helper, the Holy Spirit, whom the Father will send in My name, He will teach you all things, and bring to your remembrance all things that I said to you."

It is through that small quiet voice that we learn to walk in the realm which we cannot see. When we understand that we are in a battle, we will face trials like never before. As long as satan can convince us that there is no spiritual realm, we will remain defeated. However, once we engage in the battles at hand, we will find ourselves walking through the storms. Elijah walked through the storms, but notice, God not only allowed the storms but sent him into the midst of the storms.

1 Kings 19:11-13 (NIV) ¹¹ The LORD said, "Go out and stand on the mountain in the presence of the LORD, for the LORD is about to pass by." Then a great and powerful wind tore the mountains apart and shattered the rocks before the LORD, but the LORD was not in the wind. After the wind there was an earthquake, but the LORD was not in the earthquake. ¹² After the earthquake came a fire, but the LORD was not in the fire. And after the fire came a gentle whisper. ¹³ When Elijah heard it, he pulled his cloak over his face and went out and stood at the mouth of the cave...

God never meant us to remain in our storms. The reason for storms in the first place is to shake things up a bit. Storms in the natural are sometimes so fierce, that they take things away and even add new things. I taught a lesson on perfect storms sometime back and one illustration I gave was the volcanic eruption of 1883 that sunk two thirds of the Krakatoa Island, killing tens of thousands of lives. There were tsunamis that followed this eruption, and the massive amount of material deposited by this natural disaster dramatically altered the ocean floor surrounding the island and significantly increased the land mass of its neighboring islands. A more recent eruption has since created another island that is called Anak Krakatau, meaning **child of Krakatau**.[1]

We are able to see that because of the storm, there were things taken away and things added. The neighboring islands gained more land mass and Kratatau had less. On the second eruption, we see a whole new island was created. When we look at this in a spiritual sense, we are able to understand that storms in our lives are God's way of removing things from our lives either in the natural or things within (the spiritual), and He also adds to our lives. God ultimately knows what we need and what we do not need. The Holy Spirit was sent into our lives to do this cleanup process. As we submit to the Holy Spirit and allow the necessary changes within our lives, we will begin to see how we walk through the storms and not remain in them. As we walk through the fires unblemished, through the waters without being drowned, and through all that the enemy throws our way without being shaken, the Holy Spirit will build a whole new spiritual being, and we will be called a **child of God**.

Christians today do not always understand the power that we have through Jesus Christ because if they did, their prayer life would drastically change.

John 4:24 (NIV) [24] *"God is spirit, and his worshipers must worship in the Spirit and in truth."*

We are told that we MUST worship in the Spirit and in Truth. We know that Jesus Christ was the Word made flesh and that the Word of God is the TRUTH. If we are to be God's worshipers, we must learn how to live in the Spirit and in the Truth. In doing this, we must totally submit to God's will and learn to obey the Holy Spirit. There is no other way to be followers of Jesus Christ but through obedience. Those that are called by God must be submitted to God. The Word tells us that many are called but few are chosen.

Matthew 22:10-14 (NLV) [10] "The servants went out into the roads and brought all they could find, both bad and good. The wedding supper room was full of people. [11] The king came in to see those who had come. He saw one man who did not have on wedding supper clothes. [12] He said to him, 'Friend, how did you get in here without wedding supper clothes?' The man could not speak! [13] Then the king said to his servants, 'Tie his hands and feet, and throw him out into the darkness. In that place there will be loud crying and grinding of teeth.' [14] For many are called but few are chosen."

I have heard many teaching on this Scripture, but it is very clear. If you go back to the beginning of the teaching, the original invitation went out to a group of people that rejected the invite for whatever reason. Therefore, we get to the part where the second invitations went out beginning in verse 10.

The servants were to go out and invite all that would attend. It did not matter who they were – bad or good. The original people would have been the Jews, God's chosen, but since they rejected Jesus Christ, all others were invited to the wedding feast. Jesus uses this parable to show that there will only be few that will be chosen. There are two things Jesus shows us – first, we see that because of God's chosen people rejecting Him, salvation was for everyone. The second thing He shows us is that it is not enough to just be called or just to be invited. We are all called but few chosen. He uses one man to make His point. This one man was not chosen because of disobedience. It was evident that the man thought he could get away with being accepted at the wedding feast coming just as he was. He saw no need in making any necessary changes within his life. Yes, we are all called and Jesus welcomes us just as we are, but the time comes when we must make changes if we are to be chosen. Many today go to church weekly but do very little to change their lives throughout the week, and the Lord shows us the man in this parable did nothing to prepare and be ready for the wedding feast. We are told to watch and be ready for the second coming of Jesus Christ. We are told that our lamps must be full of oil.

Yes, many and many are called, but it will not be those that were called that come to the wedding feast. Being called is the same thing as being invited. Because of the Jews rejection to Jesus Christ, all were invited at that point. However, it is clear that only the few will be chosen. The wedding feast will only consist of those that are chosen because of their obedience. They prepared and were ready when the Lord returned for the bride. To clarify, yes, we are all disobedient at times. When we first come to the Lord, we do come just as we are. Jesus paid the price for our sins; however, we also have a bible full of stories that are to teach us how to run this race in which Paul spoke of. We cannot just continue on a path of sin and disobedience once we make the decision to follow Jesus. If we are making the decision to follow Him, then that means that we are FOLLOWING HIM! We follow in His footsteps. How often do we see small children put on their parents shoes trying to walk in their shoes? This symbolizes that if we are in love with Jesus, we are coming as small children and our desire is to wear His shoes. Jesus tells us that unless we come as children, we will not see the Kingdom of Heaven.

Matthew 18:2-3 (NIV) ² He called a little child to him, and placed the child among them. ³ And he said: "Truly I tell you, unless you change and become like little children, you will never enter the kingdom of heaven."

In order to fall in love with Jesus takes getting to know Him. We learn of Him through the Holy Spirit. We become obedient and submit unto that small voice that will lead us into the still waters. He will comfort us when we need comforting. He will wipe away our tears. He will forgive us over and over and over again. However, it comes down to a heart issue because He also knows if we are playing church.

This life is not our own. We were bought for a price and we must literally lay our lives at the cross and submit unto the Father's will. It is not about being conformed to this world but about storing treasures for the world to come. We all have a special calling upon our lives. Whether you are a parent or a teacher being obedient and pouring into our young children, these lessons are about planting the seeds that sprout and carry on into a lifetime of obedience for those that we touch. It is a huge commitment when we step out to say, *"Lord, send me and use me!"* However, it is also very rewarding knowing that the lives you are allowed to influence for just a short-time may go on to be great warriors for God's army.

Before we get started on this brilliant journey as an instructor to teach our children how to be Warriors in God's Army, I would like to share a few more things to enlighten you as a leader for those that you are blessed to impart the Word of God. An example that I have used many times for those that I minister to in regards to prayer is this, if we really believed we were in a battle, our prayers would drastically change. Our men and women who are at war, IN THE NATURAL, while in the battle field, they do not awaken at daylight praying, *"Lord, make my spouse understand me; please provide the funds I need today; change my boss so my day is good; awaken my children so they are not lazy; I need you to bless me with a car, a better job, a more understanding husband/wife, etc. etc."* Here is the deal, when they awaken knowing they are going into the midst of a real battle that day, I am assuming their prayers are focused on the battle at hand. Meaning, if you really knew that you were waking up to fight a battle which could bring you down, destroy your children, your loved ones, change your future and that of those you love, or that it might be your last day on this earth – your prayers would not be weak, they would not be empty, or about, *"What's in it for me God?"* As Americans, we have never known what it must feel like to live in a country that is plagued with war. In those countries, life does not continue as normal when bombs are going off on a daily basis. I doubt very seriously if families living in a bomb shelter, in order to keep their children alive, wake up each morning praying self-centered prayers. In America, we need to think about this when we go before God with our requests.

Most people pray when they are in the midst of a battle because they recognize they need God to rescue them, but what they fail to see is that they are in the midst of a battle daily. The majority of Christians today do nothing until they feel the pressure. If we would stay prepared, when the pressures come, we would be able to walk through as a warrior, not as someone who feels defeated. If we would stay prepared, we would be imparting a life with Jesus to our children and not a life about this world.

Let me clarify, if we are staying prepared and watching at all times for the second coming of Jesus Christ, our life would be an example to our children. Far too often, Christians today look no different than the world. We are told to present our bodies as a living sacrifice acceptable to God and also not to be conformed to this world.

Romans 12:1-2 (ESV) A Living Sacrifice [1]I appeal to you therefore, brothers, by the mercies of God, to present your bodies as a living sacrifice, holy and acceptable to God, which is your spiritual worship. ² Do not be conformed to this world, but be transformed by the renewal of your mind, that by testing you may discern what is the will of God, what is good and acceptable and perfect.[

The Scriptures tell us that our bodies should be a living sacrifice and it is through living holy that we connect with God in spiritual worship. Worship should be a daily part of our lives as we seek God and allow the Holy Spirit access. This way we would live free from sin and free from the conformities of this world. What does it look like being conformed to this world? Do we even consider this in our lives or do we just assume that we are different than the world because we go to church? We are told repeatedly to consider our ways in Haggai. But, do we consider our ways? Do we live daily to please God or are we more concerned with living to make our place in this world?

Haggai 1:3-7 (ESV) ³ Then the word of the LORD came by the hand of Haggai the prophet, ⁴ "Is it a time for you yourselves to dwell in your paneled houses, while this house lies in ruins?" ⁵ Now, therefore, thus says the LORD of hosts: Consider your ways. ⁶ You have sown much, and harvested little. You eat, but you never have enough; you drink, but you never have your fill. You clothe yourselves, but no one is warm. And he who earns wages does so to put them into a bag with holes. ⁷ "Thus says the LORD of hosts: Consider your ways."

If we call ourselves Christians then our bodies are not our own. Your body becomes the very temple in which the Holy Spirit lives.

1 Corinthians 6:19-20 (ESV) [19] Or do you not know that your body is a temple of the Holy Spirit within you, whom you have from God? You are not your own, [20] for you were bought with a price. So glorify God in your body.

Now, let's look at the world in a few different scenarios and see how others look. There are families that do not go to church, and they may live pretty good lives with the parents having college educations, making a good living, nice home and cars, and well-mannered children. Their children are involved in sports activities; they never miss attending their favorite team's games whether in person or on television; they all have their favorite sitcoms that they watch weekly; they keep up with the latest fashions in clothing as well as other items of interest; they have pensions and insurance ready for whatever comes, their treasures are stored on earth and it all seems pretty good at present. Then there are those that do not go to church that are single parent homes which are broken due to various reasons such as addictions, adultery, etc. This family doesn't know Jesus but needs Jesus. However, this family like the family that is comfortable in this world, they also strive to live storing up treasures in this world. The only difference is that this family struggles to live above their means because the picture painted especially in America is to have the American dream. The American dream desires to have the riches of this world and to keep up with the Jones', so to speak. Then there are those families that go to church and really believe in Jesus because their lives portray actions of a Christian life not just words. However, the majority of people today, especially in America, live a life aimed at gaining the indulgences of this world. I'm not going to go into a lot of detail here and I'm not going to say that it is a sin to have things in this world. I know there are many messages out there that proclaim that God will bless us with riches; however, I will add a few things, and it is up to the individual to seek God on truth.

Items to ponder...

1) The bible tells us that few will find the pathway that leads to heaven. Who are the few?
2) Jesus clearly came to define the church and in doing so, walking the same walk that He taught His disciples and all that would come after them, it is clear to see that the New Testament reflects a different mission than those in the Old Testament. As the church, what is our mission?
3) Pertaining to the church, how many followers of Jesus Christ were blessed with riches and wealth of this world?
4) If satan's job is to lead the many astray and he comes as a wolf in sheep clothing, does a

sheep look like God, sound like God, seem to be God?

5) To be trained as a warrior takes transforming our minds to think like Jesus. In doing this, we would have to also be able to recognize that which is not God. If you were the enemy, satan, what would be the easiest way to blind the eyes of Christians?

Being a leader to our children is a great responsibility but it mainly involves teaching them truth. I am a mother and a grandmother. When I leave this world, the only thing I desire to leave behind is the legacy that my children and grandchildren knew that I did not play church and my walk with Jesus Christ was very real. I want them to know that I did test the spirits anytime I sat in a church service. I want them to know that I did not believe anything I heard or anything I read unless I knew the Scriptures and the Truth. I want them to know that there is only one way to heaven and that way is not always the pleasant path. In fact, the narrow path that leads to heaven will usually look more like the path that Paul walked or the path that John walked, etc. If we are claiming to be on that same pathway running this race as Paul ran, there is going to be pain. However, the good thing is that we do not run it alone.

In teaching our children, it involves teaching them what the battle field is going to look like. It is not about teaching them that if they continue to live according to the bible that God is going to bless their lives with the riches of this world. Yes, they will be blessed, but the blessings come by being submissive, and the best blessings in this world are being able to see how your life touches someone else's life where they find Jesus Christ. It is not about riches of this world but about pouring riches in the form of peace, joy, wisdom, knowledge and understanding into the lives of those you are blessed to touch. Let me share something personal with you.

Like many parents out there, I wanted to see my granddaughter be in dancing lessons so I could be proud watching her at recitals dressed up adorable and parading across the stage shining for all to see. However, when she turned 6 years old, she let me know that this was not what she wanted. When she was 7 years old, she came to me upset because her aunt had told her that she should grow up and become a model. She is very beautiful with great features. When she told her aunt that she did not want to be a model, the conversation went to how much money she would make as a model. She came to me upset and said, *"Gammy, I don't care about the money. I want to grow up and be in the mission fields helping people."* At that moment, I was so proud of her. We have to stop dreaming a false dream for our children and allow God to develop their personalities into what He desires them to be. It is not about the money. It is not about fame or beauty. This life, our legacy must be all about Jesus Christ. What we impart to our children today will help shape them into soldiers for God's army tomorrow – His plan.

One last example to impart to our children is a lesson taught by the late Adrian Rogers. The lesson is found on the website of *Love Worth Finding Ministries,* and can be purchased on a CD. It is called, *"Beware the Kidnapper."*[2] Dr. Rogers teaches about the *"Dog and Bone"* principle. I'm not going to give this whole lesson because I encourage each of you to go to Dr. Roger's website and purchase the CD to gain great revelation, as I believe this is the most amazing lesson to impart to parents and teachers on training up a child in the way they should go. It goes back to the teachings of Moses. When Moses became of age, he did three things – he <u>refused</u> to be called the grandson of Pharaoh, and he <u>chose</u> to suffer the afflictions of his people because he had <u>esteemed</u> the greatness of God. As parents and teachers, we must do a whole lot of esteeming the riches of God if we want to impart to our children the difference between this world and the world to come. Moses could have had a life full of riches in this world, but he chose to live in poverty and to suffer instead with his people because he recognized that the world to come had far greater riches. This is what life is with Jesus Christ. We learn that it is far better to store our treasures in heaven than on this earth. It is not about **teaching** our children the Word of God because when they get older, someone else may teach them something different, and they may decide they prefer their teachings better than our teachings. It is about **esteeming**. The Dog Bone principle is about a dog with a bone in his mouth. You will probably get bit if you try to take away that bone. However, if you lay a big fat juicy steak next to the dog, what happens? First, he does some esteeming. He can see that the steak looks far better than his bone. He then does some choosing. He decides that he would rather have that steak than the bone. He then does some refusing. He spits the bone out and goes and takes the steak. The problem is that to our children, the world looks better to them than Jesus Christ. We have not taught them to do some esteeming on their own. Instead, we are busy trying to teach them and push our beliefs down their throat. We are busy telling them that they can't do this and that they have to do that. They are not choosing a life with Jesus but are being forced to live a life that we want them to live. The problem is that once they become of age, they will choose the life of this world. The life of this world is in reality a dry bone not a juicy steak. satan takes a dry bone and camouflages it with an outward appearance that looks good, sounds good, and therefore, must be good. That is how the wolf in sheep clothing sneaks in. They are not shown that drinking and drugs lead to broken marriages, children in foster homes, premature death, families torn apart, etc. They are not shown that adultery, abortions, premarital sex, etc. all lead to a pathway of destruction. They are not shown in the spiritual realm that satan is behind the scene on all of these things and has painted a pretty picture of all the fun in doing these things and much more. In the spiritual realm, we are able to see behind the scene that those dry bones are camouflaged with entertaining movies, secular music, video games, night clubs, secular concerts, etc. As parents and teachers, we have to begin in our own lives to remove the trash from our lives first so that we can begin portraying a life with Jesus Christ that begins in the spiritual realm and spills over into the natural realm. This life must show what the family looks like that serves the Lord Jesus Christ within the home, within the community, within our jobs, etc. Yes, it is a huge responsibility being called by God but rewarding as you are chosen for the wedding feast.

If we are to teach Spiritual Warfare, we must live and breathe it ourselves. Spiritual Warfare is being trained effectively to be a prayer warrior for God. The Lord has shown me that children are not too young to begin to learn the fundamentals of their armor, knowing what each piece means, and how to apply it to their everyday lives through prayer and walking clothed at all times.

We must remember that the last message Paul gave was for the church, and it was regarding our armor because he knew how important this aspect would be in the end times. If we are to run this race to the finish as Paul did, we must begin with our armor. In talking with parents, we are seeing that our children have spiritual battles just as much as adults. It is evident, that satan would love to take our children out or bring them to a place of defeat before they are even grown. I believe it is very important to not take this for granted but to begin teaching even small children about their armor. They need to learn what it means and how to use it effectively. I also believe that Paul used the Roman armor as a parallel to show God's children effectively how to be warriors as you will see in these teachings.

Purpose of this book: To equip our children with the necessary tools to be able to walk through their battles as warriors and learn to understand each piece of armor and how to use it effectively.

Course: These lessons are divided into two courses, Spiritual Warfare for Kids Beginners I and Spiritual Warfare for Kids Beginners II.

Ages: These lessons can be modified to teach from Pre-K and up, but I believe they are never too young to begin laying the groundwork for a spiritual life and this can be done simply by learning how to pray effectively over our small children and babies.

Christian Teachers: Lessons are outlined to be taught in a class setting with a review for each lesson to be sent home. In the parent sections, there will be guides to help teach on a child level for various topics along with more in depth teachings to generate growth within those that will be imparting these lessons to our children. These guides will be under the note from author section.

The song is geared to make these lessons fun and memorable. God designed mankind in His image and likeness. It is evident to see that He gave us a love for music, and we know that the Scriptures show us that there is music in heaven.

Colossians 3:16 (ESV) [16] Let the word of Christ dwell in you richly, teaching and admonishing one another in all wisdom, singing psalms and hymns and spiritual songs, with thankfulness in your hearts to God.

Revelation 5:9 (ESV) ⁹And they sang a new song, saying, "Worthy are you to take the scroll and to open its seals, for you were slain, and by your blood you ransomed people for God from every tribe and language and people and nation,

In fact, we also know that satan, once being Lucifer, was the most glorious angel of all, and was possibly in charge of the music in heaven as many biblical scholars believe.

Jeremiah 29:11(NKJV) "For I know the thoughts that I think toward you, says the Lord, thoughts of peace and not of evil, to give you a future and a hope."

Just as God's plans for Lucifer were for good and not for evil, His plans for us are the same.

Ezekiel 28:13-14 (NKJV) "You were in Eden, the Garden of God; every precious stone was your covering: The sardius, topaz and diamond, Beryl, onyx, and jasper, Sapphire, turquoise, and emerald with gold. The workmanship of your timbrels and pipes was prepared for you on the day you were created. You were anointed cherub who covers; I established you; you were on the holy mountain of God; you walked back and forth in the midst of fiery stones."

We can see that satan was created as the highest and most perfect of all of God's creations. God had great plans for Lucifer. He was loved by God very much, but regardless of how much God loves His creation, we are all given a choice to make decisions to either do good or to do evil. Just as God allows us our own free will, no matter if He knows we'll make the wrong choice ahead of time, He also allowed

Lucifer the choice to remain loyal to Him and enjoy the plans He had for him or to rebel and lose each precious promise to his own detriment.

Ezekiel 28:15-17 (NKJV)"You were perfect in your ways from the day you were created, till iniquity was found in you. By the abundance of your trading you became filled with violence within, and you sinned; Therefore I cast you as a profane thing out of the mountain of God; and I destroyed you o covering cherub from the midst of the fiery stones. Your heart was lifted up because of your beauty; you corrupted your wisdom for the sake of your splendor; I cast you to the ground, I laid you before kings, that they might gaze at you."

This was the beginning of sin that our own free will is based upon. When we make the choice to do good, in reality, we are choosing God's plan for our lives. satan had decided on another plan which conflicted with God's. Daily, we are given choices and our choices either brings us into union with satan or into union with God. Christians many times choose to not completely cross over to serving God, and it is referred to as straddling the fence. In reality, there is no middle line; there is no fence; there is no grey area. To God, everything is black and white. We either choose good or we choose evil. We choose life or death, light or darkness.

The Word promises that God is faithful, and He knows before we make our choice which one it will be; however, He still will allow us that free will. God wants warriors that will lay their lives down for His cause. He wants a people that are also faithful as He is faithful. He would not be God if He did not allow us to make the right choice or the wrong choice.

I Corinthians 10:13 (KJV) "There hath no temptation taken you but such as is common to man: but God is faithful, who will not suffer you to be tempted above that ye are able; but will with the temptation also make a way to escape, that ye may be able to bear it."

It is clear to see, in the world we live in today, that satan has distorted the music as a tool to bring the young and the old defeat within their lives. To be a warrior for God takes laying down our lives. In laying down our lives, this means there are many things we must let go of. We are not to be conformed to this world. In order to do this, we must recognize those things that are of this world and those things which are not. It is imperative that we replace music with godly music if we are to stand out and be different. It has nothing to do with the tunes but everything to do with the words.

Parents: It is imperative to understand that as a Christian parent, it is your job to impart to your children the Word of God. When we stand before God, we will account for how well we did on instructing our children in the ways of the Lord Jesus Christ. It is your responsibility to examine what is being fed to your children. Examine the words of the music they listen to; examine the television shows that they are watching. To train up a child means that you as a parent must know what is being fed to your children by way of the eyes and the ears.

Outline of Class

Spiritual Warfare for Kids Beginners I (SWKBI)

Younger Children – will learn the following: chorus of song and dance to song; basics about natural wars and spiritual wars; basics about prayer; basics about helmet of salvation, breastplate of righteousness and belt of truth

Older Children – will learn the following: complete song and dance to song; more in depth about natural wars and spiritual wars; more in depth about prayer; more in depth about helmet of salvation, breastplate of righteousness and belt of truth

Teachers/Parents – your method of teaching and degree will depend strongly on the age of the children.

Lesson 1

- Short clip on war *(nothing bloody)* just so that they can picture what a battle is in the natural
- Open discussion about how they believe there is a God, Jesus, Holy Spirit, devil, heaven and hell even though they cannot see them – explain how there is also a spiritual realm that exists even though they cannot see it
- Open discussion about spiritual battles

- Brief example about armor and why we pray to clothe ourselves with each piece

Song and dance steps – 20 minutes

Lesson 2

- Review on natural battle and spiritual battle
- Pray to equip armor brief
- Open discussion on helmet salvation and visual of Roman helmet

Song and dance steps – 20 minutes

Lesson 3

- Review on spiritual battle and helmet
- Pray to equip armor brief
- Open discussion on breastplate of righteousness and visual of Roman breastplate

Song and dance steps – 20 minutes

Lesson 4

- Review on spiritual battle, helmet and breastplate
- Pray to equip armor brief
- Open discussion on belt of truth and visual of belt

Song and dance steps – 20 minutes

Spiritual Warfare for Kids Beginners II (SWKBII)

Younger Children – will learn the following: chorus of song and dance to song; brief review on natural wars, spiritual wars, prayer, helmet of salvation, breastplate of righteousness and belt of truth; basics about gospel shoes, shield of faith, and sword of spirit

Older Children – will learn the following: chorus of song and dance to song; review on natural wars, spiritual wars, prayer, helmet of salvation, breastplate of righteousness and belt of truth; more in depth about gospel shoes, shield of faith, and sword of spirit

Lesson 1

- Review natural and spiritual wars, prayer, helmet of salvation, breastplate of righteousness and belt of truth
- Open discussion/Questions & Answers
- Pray to equip armor brief

Song and dance steps – 20 minutes

Lesson 2

- Pray to equip armor more detailed
- Open discussion on gospel shoes

Song and dance steps – 20 minutes

Lesson 3

- Review gospel shoes
- Pray to equip armor brief
- Open discussion on shield of faith

Song and dance steps – 20 minutes

Lesson 4

- Review gospel shoes and shield of faith
- Pray to equip armor brief
- Open discussion on sword of spirit

Song and dance steps – 20 minutes

PARENTS GUIDE "SONG"

Please help your child learn the Spiritual Warfare Song below. (accompaniment music can be bought through i-tunes)

Song Lyrics
(Sung to the tune – We Will Rock You)

(2 BEATS)

MOMMA ALWAYS TOLD ME TO PRAY REAL HARD

DO THE RIGHT THING AND LIVE FOR GOD

I'M A WARRIOR FOR LIFE – FOR JESUS CHRIST

FIGHTING THE DEVIL WITH ALL MY MIGHT

** WE WILL WE WILL STOMP YOU *(3 TIMES)*

~

NOW LISTEN REAL CLOSE TO WHAT I SAY

WALK THRU YOUR BATTLES WITH YOUR SHIELD OF FAITH

GOD REIGNS FOREVER AND AS HIS CREATION

I'M RUNNING THIS RACE WITH MY HELMET OF SALVATION

** WE WILL WE WILL STOMP YOU *(3 TIMES)*

~

NOW THE DEVIL IS A LIAR, DON'T BE FOOLED

STRAP ON YOUR ARMOR WITH THE BELT OF TRUTH

THE DEVIL WILL SHOOT AS WE CONFESS

WE GOT THE BREAST PLATE OF RIGHTEOUSNESS

** WE WILL WE WILL STOMP YOU *(3 TIMES)*

~

SATAN ATTACKS BUT HE'S HELL BOUND

WITH MY SWORD OF THE SPIRIT I WILL BRING HIM DOWN

GOT GOD ON MY SIDE AND I CAN'T LOSE

STOMPIN THE DEVIL WITH MY GOSPEL SHOES

** WE WILL WE WILL STOMP YOU *(3 TIMES)*

~

Dance

The dance steps can be your own creation. If possible, either purchase costumes or allow a time for a craft project to make their costume with the necessary armor pieces as this will help to come up with an original dance as the children actually lift their swords and shields. Of course, on the part "We will stomp you," this is the time for the children to STOMP! Remember, warriors are not timid and weak but bold and strong through Jesus Christ. We take authority over the enemy and all demonic forces as they are at our feet, and this can be shown in how well we reflect the words to this song.

Example Prayer for Armor

Father, we come before You this day to bring You honor and glory. We come with thanksgiving in our heart for this is the day that You have made, and we shall be glad in it. Holy Spirit, come down upon each of us and fill us with Your presence as we welcome You into our lives. Thank You, Jesus, that You sent the Comforter to walk with us each day in order to teach us all things and remind us of all truths.

Thank you Lord for the HELMET of SALVATION! We apply it to our lives this day. We put on that helmet in order that it covers our mind, having the mind of Christ as we daily renew our thoughts to Your thoughts and our ways become Your ways. We thank you Lord that the Helmet protects our eyes that we choose daily not to look upon those things which are contrary to Your Word but rather to look upon that which is good in choosing what we will watch on television and any other source of media and what we shall read that all which we do brings glory unto You and keeps our heart pure by what goes into our bodies will produce a pure heart. We thank you that our ears are covered that what we choose to listen to also brings You glory. Our mouths are covered by Your helmet that what proceeds from our lips speak faith and life not doubt and death. Our throats are protected as our choices are pure that the enemy or this world can no longer strangle the life out of us for we know that You alone are God and there is nothing that the enemy or man can do to us to bring harm or destruction even to these mortal bodies.

We thank you Lord as we apply the breastplate of righteousness knowing that our hearts are pure based on keeping our helmets in place. Our reasoning and thinking lines up with Your Word so that our hearts are not controlled based on man's ways but Yours. Place within our hearts the desires to do good and break our hearts for what breaks Yours. Let us go forth as Disciples for Jesus Christ that our love for mankind will always be nice. Give us the understanding when it comes to Your Ways that we gain love for others more than for ourselves.

We apply the Belt of Truth to the core of our existence as we study in depth Your Word above all. We seek You diligently through Your Word as we store the treasures of Your ways deep within that no one can take our knowledge away. Give us the hunger that is never fulfilled as we daily seek the Bread of Life that only Your Word can fill.

We thank you Lord as we put on our Gospel Shoes giving to others what You have given to us. We go forth as warriors proclaiming the Good News sharing the second coming of Jesus for You. Lead us not into temptation but deliver us from evil as we run this race faithfully trusting in You. Let us be the light among darkness that all will be able to see, Jesus lives in us and will live in them too. Open the doors that leads to our call and close those doors so we do not fall.

Fully clothed in our armor, we lift our shield to protect us from danger by faith in Your Will. Laying our lives at the Cross, we choose Your ways as we are ready for battle with our sword in hand. We charge forward with a cause recognizing the enemy but knowing You are with us in every battle that we face.

Thank You Lord for the angels camped about us as they battle with us each and every day. Keep Your Word in our heart that it comes out of our mouth so the enemy recognizes that we will win this bout.

SPIRITUAL WARFARE FOR KIDS BEGINNERS I

Spiritual Warfare for Kids Beginners I
LESSON 1

ALL AGES TOGETHER – Watch small clip on war
(Find a short clip showing natural war – nothing bloody but to understand war)

(Words to Song needs to be posted on wall and sent home)

Younger kids/Older kids

Go over lyrics to first chorus of song.
(This is without music – phase in the music as they learn the song)

Verse One of Song
MOMMA ALWAYS TOLD ME TO PRAY REAL HARD
DO THE RIGHT THING AND LIVE FOR GOD
I'M A WARRIOR FOR LIFE, FOR JESUS CHRIST
FIGHTING THE DEVIL WITH ALL MY MIGHT
** WE WILL WE WILL STOMP YOU (3 Times)

   PLEASE NOTE: After each lesson there is a parent review instruction sheet to be sent home with each child; however, if you are a parent teaching this, you will use both the lesson and the parent guide. The answers to these questions are only on the parent's guide which gives us the main focus on our aim to impart these lessons to our children. Although, as Christians that hear and heed the voice of the Holy Spirit, there may be additional concepts that you, as a teacher or parent, may wish to use in clarifying the answers. Please use this as a guide only for growing and shaping warriors for Jesus Christ and allow the Holy Spirit to lead you fully in order that those you are imparting God's Word receive all that our Lord and Savior would have them receive.

Open discussion...

- What is prayer?
- What is praying hard?
- Choice to do what is right or wrong/living for God
- A soldier in battle/warrior for Christ – discussing the war clip
- What are our battles? *(Discuss about things that make them sad, angry, etc.)*
- Spiritual Realm – cannot see but it is real
- How do we fight the devil? *(Brief about armor)*
- Why do we stomp on satan? *(All power of the enemy is under our feet)*

Romans 16:20 (AMP) [20]And the God of peace will soon crush Satan under your feet. The grace of our Lord Jesus Christ (the Messiah) be with you.

Luke 10:19 (AMP) [19]Behold! I have given you authority and power to trample upon serpents and scorpions, and [physical and mental strength and ability] over all the power that the enemy [possesses]; and nothing shall in any way harm you.

ALL AGES TOGETHER

Begin learning song and dance steps – send home with each child the song and lyrics along with Parent Review hand out.

PARENTS
(Detailed)
Please review lesson with your child
Spiritual Warfare for Kids Beginners I
LESSON 1 REVIEW

Verse One of Song
MOMMA ALWAYS TOLD ME TO PRAY REAL HARD
DO THE RIGHT THING AND LIVE FOR GOD
I'M A WARRIOR FOR LIFE, FOR JESUS CHRIST
FIGHTING THE DEVIL WITH ALL MY MIGHT
** WE WILL WE WILL STOMP YOU (3 Times)

SUMMARY – PRAYER ~ THE SPIRITUAL REALM ~ AUTHORITY OVER SATAN

What is prayer?

Main Focus – Intimate Relationship with God

Impartation – Prayer is merely communication in all of its forms – talking, praising, worshiping, reverence, asking, seeking, knocking, singing a new song, sharing Jesus with others, giving our testimonies, crying out to Him who cares for us and praying God's Word which has power over all circumstances.

Note from author – God is our Father and as children, we can cry out to our DAD and we can call

Him Father, Dad, Papa God, etc. Our children need to be shown just how much God loves them and yearns for their attention. It is communication with our Father as if we could see Him sitting right next to us because He is there, and He does listen and hear all that we say. It can be simple communication all day long as you share your life with the One that cares for you. As you laugh regarding all those silly things that you do, He laughs with you. God created us in His likeness and image which includes our personalities. God gave each one of us a unique personality and just like Him, we have emotions too. God does laugh; He does get angry, and there are things which make Him sad because He desires that WE know Him intimately! In this lesson, we can discuss the importance of speaking to God the Father, Jesus the Son, and the Holy Spirit. We cannot separate them because they are all One and long for us to be One with them. Your children should learn that no prayer is wrong because there are many kinds of prayers and the most important thing is that we learn to just pray and as we grow in prayer, the Holy Spirit will teach us how to pray in a way that will move heaven. This kind of prayer is praying hard which is exactly what we would do if we found ourselves in a natural war, so it only makes sense that we should do this as well in a spiritual battle.

What is praying hard?

Main Focus – What comes out of our mouth matters and speaking it with authority will move those mountains in our lives.

An example to use: if there was a situation where a stranger was bringing harm to one of your children in front of you, what would be the reaction from you the parent? The parent would not say in a calm voice, *"Stop hurting my child."* No, the parent's voice would probably be very loud towards the stranger as they came running towards their child to attack with force.

Impartation – Praying hard only happens when you understand how powerful prayer can be when it is done accurately. Praying hard only happens when you realize that all things are only possible through Christ. We cannot make things happen, but we can move heaven if we become diligent in our prayers – meaning we do not give up! Our children need to understand that our own words can do nothing to change our circumstances or to get us through a storm in life, but God's Word has power over all circumstances. Our children must learn as warriors, in order to win our battles in the spiritual realm takes leaning on God's understanding not our own.

Proverbs 3:5-6 (NLT) ⁵ Trust in the L<small>ORD</small> with all your heart; do not depend on your own understanding. ⁶ Seek his will in all you do, and he will show you which path to take.

Note From Author – There may be times that we do not understand certain situations that we are living in or problems that we face, but we trust that God is still in control. We will always encounter trouble in this life but through Jesus, we can overcome. Jesus overcame satan in the desert only because His words were that of His Father, *"It is written...."* The vision we need to impart to our children is one of authority. Through Jesus, we have authority over all circumstances in this world, but we must learn how to use that authority. Just as a parent can use that certain voice that moves their children to obey, we all have that certain voice that causes things to move. As a warrior on the battle field, we have to remember that our enemy, daily, is trying to destroy us and those that we love. Spiritual warfare is about using the voice God gave us along with His Word, not our own in order to move heaven in a way that satan has no power over us. Your tone of voice will determine if you really believe that Jesus has given you the authority to stir things up. We can walk through this life accepting those things which are uncomfortable or we can run this race as Paul shaking the very ground that we tread. As a warrior, we should go forward determined in our mind that no matter how small we are, it is through Jesus Christ that we take a stand for that which is good.

Luke 10:18-20 (NLV) [18] *Jesus said to them, "I saw Satan fall from heaven like lightning.* [19] *Listen! I have given you power to walk on snakes. I have given you power over small animals with a sting of poison. I have given you power over all the power of the one who works against you. Nothing will hurt you.* [20] *Even so, you should not be happy because the demons obey you but be happy because your names are written in heaven."*

Choice to do what is right or wrong/living for God

Main Focus – Your life and the choices you make will determine your tomorrow.

Impartation – Our children need to understand that knowingly committing sin, doing those things which are wrong, affects our prayers. Sin separates us from God and once separated, we become defeated in the spiritual realm. Our battles are lost! We live for God by striving to do what is right and communication. This would be running towards God when we miss it not away from Him due to shame. We are all on a journey in this life. There are only two roads that can be traveled. One road leads to hell and the other one leads to heaven. There is no in between just as there is no straddling the fence.

Matthew 7:13-14 (NLV) Jesus Teaches about Two Roads [13] *"Go in through the narrow door. The door is wide and the road is easy that leads to hell. Many people are going through that door.* [14] *But the door is narrow and the road is hard that leads to life that lasts forever. Few people are finding it."*

Note From Author – Your salvation is a life journey. In this life, everyone will make wrong choices. There is no such thing as living a life where you never sin. As long as we live in these earthly vessels, we will miss it. Your salvation is not determined by how many times you sin or do not sin, but it is determined by your heart. David was a man after God's own heart because he was also a man with a right heart attitude. David's mistakes were many but in his heart was a man that longed to please God. Our love for God will determine what lies deep within our hearts. God will allow storms into our lives for our own good in order to transform our hearts. It will be in those very storms that He is able to awaken us to truths in order to save our soul. We must embrace our storms knowing that these are the very things that will either keep us defeated or bring us victory. Many of the children of Israel died in the desert because they did not embrace the storm. Those that walked out of the desert learned valuable lessons about trusting God. Our God is always in control and always has a greater plan. When we are thankful instead of complaining in our storms, we will see the other side. Daily, you choose whom you will serve, but we must fully understand that one road leads to death and the other to life.

Paul said that he WAS running the race. As he came towards the end of his race, he said that he had finished it well, and the crown of life awaited him. However, while Paul was preaching one day, he claimed that he had to keep his own body disciplined, trained to do what it should because otherwise, even though he witnessed to others about Jesus Christ, he still feared that he would be disqualified if he himself did not stay fit.

1 Corinthians 9:24-27 (NLT) ²⁴Don't you realize that in a race everyone runs, but only one person gets the prize? So run to win! ²⁵ All athletes are disciplined in their training. They do it to win a prize that will fade away, but we do it for an eternal prize. ²⁶ So I run with purpose in every step. I am not just shadowboxing. ²⁷ I discipline my body like an athlete, training it to do what it should. Otherwise, I fear that after preaching to others I myself might be disqualified.

Our life journey with Jesus is not just about doing things for Him. Works will get us nowhere. How much we know about the bible will not save us. In this journey, there are going to be times that we will miss it, but it is about continuing the race and not quitting. There is no crown awaiting those that quit. There is no crown awaiting those that are disqualified. Your choices in this life will determine the outcome of where you spend eternity. The good news is that even though we stumble, if we are in a close relationship with Our Lord and Savior, we will not fall.

Psalm 37:23-24 (NLT) [23] The LORD directs the steps of the godly. He delights in every detail of their lives. [24] Though they stumble, they will never fall, for the LORD holds them by the hand.

When you stumble, you shake it off and continue the race. In a race, you are always running forward. I can't remember ever seeing a race where they ran backwards. Continuing on this journey is all about your heart attitude. A right heart attitude will cry out to God when you miss it. A right heart attitude will be one like David that has no desire to go backwards in life but to continue striving for that crown which lay before us. A warrior never backs down but continues on a forward course to win.

We must remember that if we are in communication with God, He has us in His hands. David lived for God but was a sinner, and God said of David, *"This is a man after my own heart."* God loved David because of what was in his heart. We have strengths in our lives as well as weaknesses, but it comes down to what is in our heart. David was weak in areas, but he cried out to God because this was not who he wanted to be. David loved God dearly and God recognized His weaknesses. Man looks at the outer but God looks at the heart.

1 Samuel 16:7 (NLT) ⁷ But the LORD said to Samuel, "Don't judge by his appearance or height, for I have rejected him. The LORD doesn't see things the way you see them. People judge by outward appearance, but the LORD looks at the heart."

Your choices in life will determine what is in your heart. When you choose continually to do the same thing which is contrary to God's Word, you are trying to use your own strength to overcome. We can overcome all things but only through Him that gives us strength. We will never overcome our weaknesses through ourselves. To live for God means to die to self. It is adapting to the desires of Jesus Christ not of this world. Our desires for this world will only change as we draw closer to Him as He calls us. Many are called but few chosen and that is only because the many choose to live as this world, conformed to this world. The few have found something far greater just as Moses did. Moses chose rather than to live a life of luxury, to live in poverty with his people because he had esteemed the riches of God.

Hebrews 11:24-27 (NLT) ²⁴ It was by faith that Moses, when he grew up, refused to be called the son of Pharaoh's daughter. ²⁵ He chose to share the oppression of God's people instead of enjoying the fleeting pleasures of sin. ²⁶ He thought it was better to suffer for the sake of Christ than to own the treasures of Egypt, for he was looking ahead to his great reward. ²⁷ It was by faith that Moses left the land of Egypt, not fearing the king's anger. He kept right on going because he kept his eyes on the one who is invisible.

Your children will only esteem the riches of God based on what they see in your own heart. If your life is filled with riches of this world and your desires outside of church are filled with conforming to this world, they will only esteem this world. Jesus is our example as well as those that followed Him. It is okay to enjoy the natural beauty of this world and to partake in those desires which God instilled in each of us, but our focus in this world must be to prepare for the second coming of Jesus Christ and to impart to others the importance of being a Disciple for Jesus. Jesus should be with us at church, home, school, the workplace, vacations, etc. Your choices will be what you impart to your children or those that you have a great influence over.

Soldier in battle/Warrior for Christ

Main Focus – We are in a battle every day, but we are all called to be warriors for Jesus Christ.

Impartation – Your child saw a short clip on war *(nothing bloody)* in order to understand about natural war. This was to help them with a visual of war, so they can begin to understand there is another war which cannot be seen. Your child is learning that this war *(the spiritual realm)* goes on all around them and affects things in this natural world, but through Jesus, they are learning that they have the power to overcome and walk through their battles as victors!

Note From Author – God created us body, soul and spirit. Very little is taught about our spirit-man even within the church. It is imperative that our children at a young age become familiar with the complete makeup of man. Christians today that live a victorious life recognize that in order to do so takes knowledge in all things spiritual. God tells us that we perish from lack of knowledge.

Hosea 4:6 (ESV) ⁶My people are destroyed for lack of knowledge; because you have rejected knowledge, I reject you from being a priest to me. And since you have forgotten the law of your God, I also will forget your children.

According to Peter, if we believe in Jesus Christ, we are a chosen race, a royal priesthood. However, without full knowledge of who God is, we will perish. God gave us a complete history book into the depths of just who He is. History books are designed to teach us about the past in order that we can learn from it for our future, but the Word of God is the only book that also tells us about our future. When we lack knowledge in the things of God, we will not live a victorious life in this world and will be deceived from traveling the path which leads to heaven. The many, we know travel the wide path but that is from lack of knowledge. You cannot stand before God one day for Him to say, *"Well done my faithful servant,"* when you have done nothing and when you have not been faithful. As faithful servants, we should be striving to renew our minds to think like Jesus Christ. Once our minds are on the right path, our desires should also be changing in that we want more of God. Leading our children through this world means that it begins with the parents and in the homes. Our children will only hunger after what we hunger for. Standing before God is either to KNOW HIM or to be a stranger. His words will either be, *"Depart from me for I do not know you"* or *"Well done... come on in!"*

Matthew 7:21-23 (NLT) [21] *"Not everyone who calls out to me, 'Lord! Lord!' will enter the Kingdom of Heaven. Only those who actually do the will of my Father in heaven will enter.* [22] *On judgment day many will say to me, 'Lord! Lord! We prophesied in your name and cast out demons in your name and performed many miracles in your name.'* [23] *But I will reply, 'I never knew you. Get away from me, you who break God's laws.'"*

Matthew 25:23 (AMP) [23] *His master said to him, Well done, you upright (honorable, admirable) and faithful servant! You have been faithful and trustworthy over a little; I will put you in charge of much. Enter into and share the joy (the delight, the blessedness) which your master enjoys.*

We must begin to impart the spiritual realm to our children because it is in that realm that we come to really KNOW HIM!

What are our battles?

Main Focus – Our battles are two-part, with one being our strongholds and the other being the storms.

Impartation – Our battles are storms in this life, but we can look at these in two parts. The first thing that we battle is our self. It is our fleshly desires that produce the strongholds in our lives. These are areas where we struggle inside.

Romans 7:15 (ESV) ¹⁵ For I do not understand my own actions. For I do not do what I want, but I do the very thing I hate.

Paul said that he did not do what he wanted to do but what he hated to do. We see ourselves saying, *"Lord, my flesh wants to do this but I want to do what is right."* This is the battle within. This is the area where the Holy Spirit is at work within us. Our desire is to live for God, yet, we miss it again and again because we have no control over sin when we are trying to overcome through our own strength. Much of what we do wrong produces those storms within our lives which become the second part. Sometimes the storms are due to our own will and other times the storms just happen, but there may be reasons that we do not understand. This life can be looked at as a huge puzzle and the awesome part is that we all have a place in that puzzle. There are times that we encounter huge storms but in those storms, God is still at work in our lives. Sometimes the storm can be the result of our own wrong choice and other times it may be the result of someone else's choice, but regardless, we still find ourselves in the midst of the high winds. However, we must learn to ride out the storms. How long we are in the storm can depend on our own stubbornness. Just as the children of Israel suffered in the desert, we suffer many times because God is trying to do a work within us. When our own free will fights His will for our lives, in the spiritual realm, there is a huge war engaging. Living outside of His will is going to bring destruction. The Word tells us that the wages of sin is death.

Romans 6:23 (NLT) [23]*For the wages of sin is death, but the free gift of God is eternal life through Christ Jesus our Lord.*

Note From Author – God gives us our own free will, and we can live doing as we please, but living outside of Him will never be living a life that is blessed. True blessings only come from that which is good. This means that a life that is blessed will be a life that walks with God. We can have temporary peace and joy in this life, but it will never be the same peace and joy which only come from Our Creator. Those temporary things which bring us happiness are short lived in this world. We all will come to the place, even the wealthy, where money and things no longer bring happiness. True happiness only happens within and does not need the material things in this world to produce that euphoria which our souls desire.

When our bodies are waging war within, it produces anxiety, fear, feelings of failure, defeat, anger, etc. When we are in a storm, we tend to want to find blame for our current circumstances. We are no different than the children of Israel. They blamed God and Moses for their predicament. Your child is learning that the battle is not with other people but a battle they cannot see. satan will use your storms in this life to bring you down and separate you from God, and he does this by convincing you that your situation is not your fault. Your child is learning that the most important thing is not that they are in the midst of a battle but how to walk through that battle. As warriors, they will fight their battles, but they will learn to do so as James said in James 1:2-4,*"Counting it all joy."* Our battles we walk through not only produce good things but they also mold and make us more like Christ. Your child is learning that even though they may feel defeated at times, it's about getting back up and continuing to run this race as a soldier/warrior in the ranks of the Most High God!

Spiritual Realm – cannot see but it is real

Main Focus – Two realms, one that is seen with our natural eyes and one that is seen through our spiritual eyes.

Impartation – We discussed today about how we believe that God exists, Jesus was the Son of God, the devil is real, there is a heaven and hell but even though we cannot see any of this with our natural eyes, we know it to be true. This set the stage to understand that there are many things we cannot see but we know they exist. We were created in the image and likeness of God, and we were created as spiritual beings. It is our spiritual self which connects with God, heaven, and the spiritual realm.

Note From Author – We have two sets of eyes. One sees things in the natural and the other sees things in the spiritual. If we live our lives solely around those things we can see naturally, we will live a defeated Christian life. What we cannot see is far greater and more powerful than what we can see. It is the unseen world that brings great influence to the seen world. In fact, it was God, in the unseen world, which created everything we see today. God created the world that we see by speaking it into existence with His Word. He created everything we see from nothing and all of this was done in the realm that we cannot see.

Hebrews 11:3 (NLV) ³Through faith we understand that the world was made by the Word of God. Things we see were made from what could not be seen.

Our choices in this life are greatly affected by what we cannot see. We speak and can hear our words, but we cannot see our words. Words are powerful in the spiritual realm. They can produce life or death. When we awaken each day, it is imperative that we begin the day recognizing the realm we cannot see. Remember, God said that His people perish from lack of knowledge. We must have knowledge of all things spiritually. If the spiritual realm makes the difference of what happens in our lives, we need to pay much more attention to that realm. In the spiritual realm, we cannot see God, Jesus or the Holy Spirit, but we believe they exist and with our spiritual eyes we can see them. We see in the spiritual because this realm exists deep within our own spirit. Our spirit connects with God. When we hear his voice from deep within, it is how He connects with us. When we gain revelation by reading His Word, again, it is our spirit connecting with His. In this realm, there is light and darkness that we cannot see but we know they exist. There are angels and demons, good and evil. Daily, we awaken and are in a battle whether we engage or not. Understanding the spiritual realm is all about being a warrior for Jesus Christ so that we can prepare for this battle daily. We prepare by understanding that in this realm, there is darkness that wishes to defeat us but light that protects us. If we do not connect with the light daily, we will be pulled into the darkness.

How do we fight the devil?

Main Focus – Our battles are not with flesh and blood. Our battles are not with things we can see but things we cannot see. To overcome in this world, our focus daily must be in knowing our armor and applying it to our lives. In order to know something, we gain knowledge.

Impartation – We discussed how God formed the world with His Word. We discussed how powerful our words are especially when we line them up with God's Word. Our words can bring defeat or victory. We fight the devil by putting on the whole armor of God and that is speaking it into existence. Even though we cannot see our spiritual armor, we know it is on and we are equipped to fight in the spiritual realm which we also know that we cannot see.

Note From Author – God sent His Son, Jesus, in the flesh in order to know the battles that we face daily. He came as a man, but He overcame through power from on high. That power is alive within each of us when we accept the Holy Spirit into our lives. It is important that our children understand that our enemy, satan, desires to bring them down. Most importantly, satan desires that we walk away from following the path which will lead us to heaven. Once again, most Christians today are defeated because of lack of knowledge.

If Christians today are missing heaven due to lack of knowledge, then it is important to listen to what the Scriptures tell us. The answers to anything we are going through are in the Scriptures. If people do not believe this, it is because they do not know the Scriptures. The key word here is "know." To gain knowledge about anything in this life can only be acquired by either reading or paying attention to someone as they teach you about those things you desire, and the next step would be walking in what you have learned. Even though a doctor has gained the knowledge in his head, this does not make him a doctor. He must then go through training in the field in which he has gained knowledge. Jesus expects us to go and do. Jesus gained the knowledge and then He faced satan in the desert. In the desert, the battle was won. Knowledge can be gained based on how bad we desire to be like Jesus. Knowledge is gained by pouring into the Scriptures. I do not advise anyone to just gain their knowledge by listening to someone else's relationship with God. When we listen to the man or woman at the pulpit, we are in fact listening to what they have gained by KNOWING God intimately. NO ONE will enter heaven if they do not KNOW God themselves. Once again, the *"many"* will stand before God and He will say, *"Depart from me..."*

To defeat satan and overcome this world, we must gain knowledge by studying ourselves which also develops that intimate relationship with Our Father. By doing what the Scriptures tell us, we will gain wisdom. Doing is also walking through our storms. For every single trial in this life you walk through, you will gain wisdom. One question, if you are seeking answers to a problem in your own life and you make the effort to go listen to a Christian speaker talk specifically about your situation or you are going to read a book written about what you are going through, which speaker or author would you rather listen to? Would you rather listen to the speaker or author that has gained knowledge by the Word of God or by one that has gained the knowledge by the Word of God and also they have walked through your specific situation? Walking through the storms gains the wisdom, but gaining the wisdom doesn't stop there. Once you gain the wisdom, you need the understanding. Understanding comes from God. This will be your revelation that God shows you in order that you understand the reason that you had to go through the storm in the first place. We are told by James to count it all joy for our trials.

James 1:2-4 (AMP) ²Consider it wholly joyful, my brethren, whenever you are enveloped in or encounter trials of any sort or fall into various temptations. ³ Be assured and understand that the trial and proving of your faith bring out endurance and steadfastness and patience. ⁴ But let endurance and steadfastness and patience have full play and do a thorough work, so that you may be [people] perfectly and fully developed [with no defects], lacking in nothing.

The reason to count it all joy is because of what we gain. The Scripture tells us that we gain endurance, steadfastness, and patience. Once we grow in these areas, James tells us that we will lack in nothing. When trials or storms come our way, we have two choices. One choice is to be like the children of Israel that spent 40 years in the desert because they murmured and complained while listening to the wrong voice, or we can rise above that and be like James, counting it all joy for what we are going through because by faith, we understand that God has a much greater plan for our lives. It is through these storms that we grow to become the warriors He created us to be, and as a trained warrior in the Army of God, we will have learned how to fight the enemy the same way that Jesus Christ fought Him in the desert. Remember, we do not fight with flesh and blood but by every Word which comes out of the mouth of God. We fight with all that is within us, given to us through knowledge of Our Lord and Savior as we gain wisdom and understanding by faith in Him alone. This takes living and breathing the Word of God. We will never win our battles by using mortal words or mortal wisdom. God said that the wisdom of this world is foolishness.

1 Corinthians 3:19 (NLT) [19]For the wisdom of this world is foolishness to God. As the Scriptures say, "He traps the wise in the snare of their own cleverness."

As we gain knowledge through God's Word, we also become that person that can share not just the knowledge but also the wisdom and understanding.

Why do we stomp on satan?

Main Focus – Understanding the tactics of our enemy will keep us at a place to recognize our battle through our spiritual eyes not as the world sees things.

Impartation – According to God's Word, satan is under our feet; therefore, we stomp on him to keep him in his place. We have nothing to fear because we are God's children and have been given authority over the enemy.

Romans 16:20 (AMP) [20]And the God of peace will soon crush Satan under your feet. The grace of our Lord Jesus Christ (the Messiah) be with you.

Luke 10:19 (AMP) ¹⁹Behold! I have given you authority and power to trample upon serpents and scorpions, and [physical and mental strength and ability] over all the power that the enemy [possesses]; and nothing shall in any way harm you.

Note From Author – We already know that satan is a defeated foe, but he is also running to and fro seeking whom he may devour. It is important to have understanding not just knowledge. Yes, we must have the knowledge so that we do not perish, but we should desire to have wisdom, knowledge, and understanding. If we are to become warriors for Jesus Christ, then we should desire to go through ALL of Boot Camp in order to be trained by the Holy Spirit. Jesus tells us that it was better for Him to go away because something great was coming.

John 16:5-14 (NLT) The Work of the Holy Spirit ⁵ "But now I am going away to the one who sent me, and not one of you is asking where I am going. ⁶ Instead, you grieve because of what I've told you. ⁷ But in fact, it is best for you that I go away, because if I don't, the Advocate won't come. If I do go away, then I will send him to you. ⁸ And when he comes, he will convict the world of its sin, and of God's righteousness, and of the coming judgment. ⁹ The world's sin is that it refuses to believe in me. ¹⁰ Righteousness is available because I go to the Father, and you will see me no more. ¹¹ Judgment will come because the ruler of this world has already been judged." ¹² "There is so much more I want to tell you, but you can't bear it now. ¹³ When the Spirit of truth comes, he will guide you into all truth. He will not speak on his own but will tell you what he has heard. He will tell you about the future. ¹⁴ He will bring me glory by telling you whatever he receives from me."

Jesus was able to overcome and win the battle because of power from on high as stated before. Our desires should not be just to walk through our battles but to come out of those battles unharmed physically, mentally, and emotionally. Think about the Scriptures, they tell us of Daniel and the Lion's den. They tell us about the 3 Hebrew boys – Shadrach, Meshach and Abednego, being thrown into the fire. They tell us about the children of Israel walking on dry ground as God parted the Red Sea. There are many more biblical stories, but the concept is that they were not harmed, not burned, not drowned, etc. We need to gain everything possible in order to understand the tactics of our enemy. We should be the head not the tail, above not beneath, and blessed going in and coming out. This does not mean we will not face hardship, but when hardship comes, we will still know how to keep our enemy under our feet. We should welcome the storms in our lives because your storms are your actual training in the battlefield. In natural war, medals are achieved and honor is given by those that had victory in the field of battle even if there were battle scars. Your storms are your on-hand training that will gain you awards in heaven if you allow the Holy Spirit into your life to train you in spiritual warfare. Part of your training is gaining the understanding for the purpose of any particular battle you may be facing and learning to go through it victoriously. Remember, a warrior never quits, never questions, never compromises, and never complains. Warriors run and they do not grow weary; they walk and they do not faint all the way to the finish.

*Isaiah 40:31 (NIV) ³¹ but those who hope in the L*ORD *will renew their strength. They will soar on wings like eagles; they will run and not grow weary, they will walk and not be faint.*

In doing so, warriors are always thankful and show reverence to the One that gave them life. If we desire that our children are warriors in this world, their training is a daily regimen that begins as they watch parents, Christian teachers, and leaders fulfill their own missions in which Jesus Christ has given them. A great leader leads by example. Our examples must be in showing that it is not about the battle, it is about the outcome. Even though we may get bruised, beaten, go hungry, and sometimes come to the place where we feel that we cannot continue, the final mission is achieving the goal that we set out for. As warriors, we never ever quit and never retreat. In a race, all desire to win and will go to great lengths and pain to make it to that finish line. As warriors, our eyes must stay fixed on Jesus Christ as our example to fulfilling the great calling that was placed on our lives. We do this by going forward not backwards. A winner is one that ultimately continues striving for the goal or the prize set before them and in doing so, daily, they keep the enemy under their feet!

Always remember that one of our enemy's tactics is to attack your mind by convincing you that you are not good enough. As Christians, we spend too much time listening to the wrong voice that desires to rise up in our lives and keep us under his control. To counter this attack of fiery darts, we must learn that if the voice doesn't sound like Jesus, it probably is not Jesus. You have the authority at that moment to declare, *"satan, you are a defeated foe, get thee behind me because I refuse to listen to anything you have to say!"* When you can't silence that voice, begin praising the One that gave you life. satan hates to hear the name of Jesus being exalted. Praise and worship is the greatest form of spiritual warfare and when you find yourself in a battle, you have the authority to silence that battle and put the enemy under your feet.

Spiritual Warfare for Kids Beginners I
LESSON 2

ALL AGES TOGETHER – Visual of Roman Armor *(have two sets for each group)*

Show each piece of armor briefly – will be discussing helmet today

Ephesians 6:10-17 (ESV)
The Whole Armor of God
¹⁰Finally, be strong in the Lord and in the strength of his might. ¹¹ Put on the whole armor of God, that you may be able to stand against the schemes of the devil. ¹²For we do not wrestle against flesh and blood, but against the rulers, against the authorities, against the cosmic powers over this present darkness, against the spiritual forces of evil in the heavenly places. **¹³Therefore take up the whole armor of God, that you may be able to withstand in the evil day, and having done all, to stand firm. ¹⁴Stand therefore**, having fastened on the belt of truth, and having put on the breastplate of righteousness, ¹⁵and, as shoes for your feet, having put on the readiness given by the gospel of peace. ¹⁶In all circumstances take up the shield of faith, with which you can extinguish all the flaming darts of the evil one; **¹⁷and take the helmet of salvation,** and the sword of the Spirit, which is the word of God,

Pray to equip armor brief

(Divide Groups)

(Words to Song will be posted on wall and sent home for any new kids)

Younger kids/Older kids

Will go over lyrics to second chorus of song.
(This is without music – end of lesson will be music)

Verse Two of Song
NOW LISTEN REAL CLOSE TO WHAT I SAY
WALK THRU YOUR BATTLES WITH YOUR SHIELD OF FAITH
GOD IS FOREVER AND I'M HIS CREATION
RUN THIS RACE WITH YOUR HELMET OF SALVATION
** WE WILL WE WILL STOMP YOU (3 TIMES)

Review on natural battle and spiritual battle

- In song it says that we walk through our battles
- Reminder, what are our battles

Open discussion on helmet salvation…

- What is salvation?
- What are we actually doing when we place that helmet on our head? *(Pick one child each group to come forward to place helmet on their head)*
- What does the helmet cover?
    - *It covers our brain which is our mind, why should we cover our mind? Mind of Christ – thoughts, feelings, purposes*

- *It covers our eyes and ears, why should we cover them? So they are open to truth and not deceived by lies*
- *It guards our mouth, why should we guard our mouth? What comes forth from our mouth should glorify God, edify and encourage others, and speak forth power to move our mountains and fulfill our purpose for God*

ALL AGES TOGETHER

Song – work on and dance steps *(20 minutes)* – send home with any new kids the song/lyrics and all kids the Parent Review for Lesson 2.

PARENTS
(Detailed)
Please review lesson with your child
Spiritual Warfare for Kids Beginners I
LESSON 2 REVIEW

Verse Two of Song
NOW LISTEN REAL CLOSE TO WHAT I SAY
WALK THRU YOUR BATTLES WITH YOUR SHIELD OF FAITH
GOD IS FOREVER AND I'M HIS CREATION
RUN THIS RACE WITH YOUR HELMET OF SALVATION
** WE WILL WE WILL STOMP YOU (3 TIMES)

Ephesians 6:10-17 (ESV)

The Whole Armor of God

10Finally, be strong in the Lord and in the strength of his might. 11 Put on the whole armor of God, that you may be able to stand against the schemes of the devil. 12For we do not wrestle against flesh and blood, but against the rulers, against the authorities, against the cosmic powers over this present darkness, against the spiritual forces of evil in the heavenly places. **13Therefore take up the whole armor of God, that you may be able to withstand in the evil day, and having done all, to stand firm. 14Stand therefore,** having fastened on the belt of truth, and having put on the breastplate of righteousness, 15and, as shoes for your feet, having put on the readiness given by the gospel of peace. 16In all circumstances take up the shield of faith, with which you can extinguish all the flaming darts of the evil one; **17and take the helmet of salvation,** and the sword of the Spirit, which is the word of God,

SUMMARY – HELMET OF SALVATION

EMPHASIS ON GOD BEING OUR DADDY

What is salvation?

Main Focus – Salvation is gained one day at a time. Being saved is striving for the prize set before us and is granted to us by One God only! Your salvation is determined solely by your heart and that decision will come from Our Creator as you stand before Him one day. Your intimate relationship with God is totally dependent on your inward desire to KNOW HIM!

Impartation – Your child is learning what being saved means. We can teach in basic terms, if someone is drowning and another person jumps in to keep them from drowning, then that person is saved by the hero who rescued them. Jesus is our hero, and it is only through Him that we can be saved from drowning in the depths of sin. We are discussing how the devil wants us to give up and allow ourselves to drown in order to keep us away from Jesus. However, the bible says that all we have to do is cry out to God and believe His Word totally. We must believe we were created by God, and Jesus died for us. We must believe that He rose again and sits in heaven at the side of our Father, while the Holy Spirit lives within us. Salvation is for all who believe but it must be heartfelt. This is best emphasized by the feelings a child has for their parents. They believe that their parents love them and by this, they can believe that God loves them because He is their Daddy!

Note From Author – Salvation is a process, it is not as religion would have you believe, a ritual where you only need to confess Jesus as Savior or be baptized, etc. If it were that easy, we all would make it to heaven, but we know that the bible says that only the few will travel the road that leads to heaven. Now few, could mean thousands compared to the multitudes that have been born since creation, and it could mean hundreds of thousands. I prefer to not try to decipher what God meant, but rather to focus on the fact that the *"many"* would not see heaven. In this, Jesus tells us that there will be many stand before Him on that day as He says, *"Depart from me for I never knew you…,"* and He goes on to show us that they try to convince Him that they should belong in heaven because they felt they were living a Christian life.

Matthew 7:21-23 (NLT) True Disciples [21] "Not everyone who calls out to me, 'Lord! Lord!' will enter the Kingdom of Heaven. Only those who actually do the will of my Father in heaven will enter. [22] On judgment day many will say to me, 'Lord! Lord! We prophesied in your name and cast out demons in your name and performed many miracles in your name.' [23] But I will reply, 'I never knew you. Get away from me, you who break God's laws.'"

This shows us clearly that the many in which Jesus is referring to believed they were saved. Those words of reply were from those that felt they were Christians whether it was because they attended church or felt that they were doing works which warranted rewards. Jesus' reply of never knowing them has to do with a relationship and nothing more. With this in mind, our salvation comes the day we stand before Our Lord and Creator, and He either says, *"Depart" or "Well done!"* The main thing to see here is that salvation is a process just as Paul stated that he was *"being"* saved – that he was *"running"* the race, and when Paul knew his time was about up, he said that he had *"ran"* the race well.

2 Timothy 4:6-8 (NLT) ⁶As for me, my life has already been poured out as an offering to God. The time of my death is near. ⁷I have fought the good fight, I have finished the race, and I have remained faithful. ⁸And now the prize awaits me—the crown of righteousness, which the Lord, the righteous Judge, will give me on the day of his return. And the prize is not just for me but for all who eagerly look forward to his appearing.

Paul says that the crown of righteousness awaits him. This says a lot about our walk with God. Christianity becomes a way of life and as we travel that road, our goal is to run the race in the same manner as Paul. Christianity became Paul's life. Spreading the gospel became his way of life. Paul's character was one that devoted everything to serving Our Lord. Paul had ran the race well and knew he had a crown awaiting him. Salvation on the other hand is not a free gift as most religions will tell you. In fact, salvation will cost you everything, but God's grace is a gift.

Ephesians 2:8 (NLT) ⁸God saved you by his grace when you believed. And you can't take credit for this; it is a gift from God.

This merely means that it is only because of God that we can even be saved. It takes His saving grace to wipe the slate clean and erase all our sin. However, salvation is much more than just making the assumption that we are saved. To follow Jesus means letting go of your life as you know it prior to Christ.

Romans 6:5-18 (NLT) ⁵Since we have been united with him in his death, we will also be raised to life as he was. ⁶ We know that <u>our old sinful selves were crucified with Christ so that sin might lose its power in our lives.</u> We are no longer slaves to sin. ⁷ For <u>when we died with Christ we were set free from the power of sin.</u> ⁸ And since we died with Christ, we know we will also live with him. ⁹ We are sure of this because Christ was raised from the dead, and he will never die again. Death no longer has any power over him. ¹⁰ When he died, he died once to break the power of sin. But now that he lives, he lives for the glory of God. ¹¹ So you also should consider yourselves to be dead to the power of sin and alive to God through Christ Jesus.

¹² <u>Do not let sin control the way you live; do not give in to sinful desires</u>. ¹³ Do not let any part of your body become an instrument of evil to serve sin. Instead, <u>give yourselves completely to God, for you were dead, but now you have new life</u>. So use your whole body as an instrument to do what is right for the glory of God. ¹⁴ Sin is no longer your master, for you no longer live under the requirements of the law. Instead, <u>you live under the freedom of God's grace</u>.

15 Well then, <u>since God's grace has set us free from the law, does that mean we can go on sinning? Of course not!</u> 16 Don't you realize that <u>you become the slave of whatever you choose to obey? You can be a slave to sin, which leads to death, or you can choose to obey God, which leads to righteous living.</u> 17 Thank God! Once you were slaves of sin, but now you wholeheartedly obey this teaching we have given you. 18 <u>Now you are free from your slavery to sin, and you have become slaves to righteous living.</u>

Here is our crown of righteousness which Paul spoke of. Knowing he had run the race well, he was set free from being a slave to sin and he chose to live a life of righteousness. Paul did this by dying to self – dying to his desires, his wants, his ambitions and following where the Holy Spirit led him in his particular calling for his life. Jesus also tells us without righteousness, we will not enter into the Kingdom of Heaven.

Matthew 5:20 (KJV) 20For I say unto you, That except your righteousness shall exceed [the righteousness] of the scribes and Pharisees, ye shall in no case enter into the kingdom of heaven.

We need to continually ask ourselves if we are running this race well. We need to ask ourselves if our walk with God looks anything like Paul's walk. We need to ask ourselves if our relationship with Our Creator is intimate. There are 3 parts to salvation – body, soul, and spirit. Let's flip these around and begin with spirit. When you first believed in Jesus Christ, your spirit at that point was awakened because the Holy Spirit had been convicting you to a life of righteousness and sending people across your path to share Jesus Christ. This is only the first step to a life of righteousness and salvation. Jesus tells us that it is evident whose father you belong to due to your actions.

1 John 3:7-10 (NLT) ⁷ Dear children, don't let anyone deceive you about this: When people do what is right, it shows that they are righteous, even as Christ is righteous. ⁸ But when people keep on sinning, it shows that they belong to the devil, who has been sinning since the beginning. But the Son of God came to destroy the works of the devil. ⁹ Those who have been born into God's family do not make a practice of sinning, because God's life is in them. So they can't keep on sinning, because they are children of God. ¹⁰ So now we can tell who are children of God and who are children of the devil. Anyone who does not live righteously and does not love other believers does not belong to God.

If your actions are still doing things according to your fleshly desires, you are not living a life which is holy. We cannot straddle the fence. There is no grey area with God. There is good and there is evil. Our soul is our will, emotions, desires, personality, etc. Just because your spirit awakens does not mean you are where you need to be with God. Jesus tells us that we are to die to self, meaning that we crucify our flesh at the cross with Him. If we are His followers, He tells us that the world will hate us because it hated Him; we will be persecuted because we are one of His. We need to ask ourselves if we have stirred things up enough to cause division among those that we were once close to. Jesus said that He came to divide, mother against daughter, etc.

Luke 12:49-53 (NLT) Jesus Causes Division *⁴⁹ "I have come to set the world on fire, and I wish it were already burning! ⁵⁰ I have a terrible baptism of suffering ahead of me, and I am under a heavy burden until it is accomplished. ⁵¹ Do you think I have come to bring peace to the earth? No, I have come to divide people against each other! ⁵² From now on families will be split apart, three in favor of me, and two against—or two in favor and three against. ⁵³ 'Father will be divided against son and son against father; mother against daughter and daughter against mother; and mother-in-law against daughter-in-law and daughter-in-law against mother-in-law.'"*

Our soul is the second part of salvation that occurs and will only happen if we allow the Holy Spirit total access into our lives. Jesus tells us that it was better that He went away so that the Holy Spirit would come. The Holy Spirit's job is to clean house. If you allow Him access, He will begin removing things and adding things to your life, but there will be many choices you will need to make and those choices will determine if you walk a holy life or one filled with earthly desires and riches. It is in this part that your life changes and your desires change and your heart becomes one with Our Creator.

The third part of salvation is your body. This is total transformation to your new spiritual body when you stand before God and He says, *"Well done!"* At that point when you gain access into the Kingdom of Heaven, you will do so with your newly created spiritual body that will never grow old, never have pain and sorrow, and never die a spiritual death.

What are we doing when we place the helmet on our head?

Main Focus – The Helmet of Salvation should be applied daily to our lives. We are saved on a daily basis by recognizing that Jesus paid the price but it takes action on our part to remain in close relationship with our Father. There is NO ONCE SAVED ALWAYS SAVED. Salvation is not a ritual – it is a way of life!

Impartation – We discussed that we accept the helmet from Papa God – meaning we accept that Jesus died for us and because we believe, we also know we are saved. We place the helmet on our head because we know that our Daddy gave us this tool for protection, as His sons and daughters.

Note From Author – Like with any relationship, it take hard work. Your child cannot have a relationship with you (the parents) if they never communicate. Communication comes in many forms. We communicate by spending time with someone. We communicate by talking to that person, and we also communicate by listening. A relationship is two-fold. It takes at least two people and both have to be willing to work at the relationship. Your child cannot go to school and have a relationship with their teacher if they never speak, listen, or do what they are told. This relationship would be broken and the result would lead to their failure in school. The same with any relationship, without communication in all its forms, there would be no relationship, and the result is failure. Daily, most Christians reject the Lord because they never even acknowledge His presence. When we go about our day without spending time with Jesus, our life will soon show areas of failure. Relationships will crumble when there is NO GOD relationship. When a marriage leaves God out, that marriage will be weakened. When we leave God out of the equation, other relationships will weaken. God expects us to be faithful with what He has given us first before we are blessed with more. An example is that we are to be faithful with the first relationship He has given us and that would be the relationship with Jesus Christ. When we cannot be faithful in that relationship, we cannot be trusted with other relationships either. Leave God out and watch your other relationships crumble whether it be with teachers, spouses, employers, friends, other family members, etc. Seek first His Kingdom and what happens?

Matthew 6:31-33 (ESV) ³¹Therefore do not be anxious, saying, 'What shall we eat?' or 'What shall we drink?' or 'What shall we wear?' ³² For the Gentiles seek after all these things, and your heavenly Father knows that you need them all. ³³ But seek first the kingdom of God and his righteousness, and all these things will be added to you.

Therefore, if daily, upon arising, we put God first by applying our helmet to our lives, we will walk throughout our day in the goodness that God has given us. It is a way of life.

What does the helmet cover?

Main Focus – As Christians, we understand that by applying the helmet first to our lives on a daily basis, the two outlets where sin can enter are covered which is our eyes and our ears. In covering those outlets, our mind is covered to have the mind of Christ where what is in our heart that proceeds from our mouth will be good and not evil.

Impartation – We discussed how each piece of the armor in biblical days protected certain areas of the body, and Paul used this as an example in order for God's children to understand how each piece is also a tool to protect certain elements in the spiritual realm – meaning each piece of armor has its purpose and protects us in areas that could cause us to fall into temptation and evils (bad things).

Note From Author –

The helmet covers...
> 1) Our mind... so that we have the mind of Christ – we think like Jesus

1 Corinthians 2:16 (AMP) ¹⁶For who has known or understood the mind (the counsels and purposes) of the Lord so as to guide and instruct Him and give Him knowledge? But we have the mind of Christ (the Messiah) and do hold the thoughts (feelings and purposes) of His heart.

> 2) Our eyes and ears – so they are opened to truth and not deceived by lies

Acts 26:18 (AMP) ¹⁸To open their eyes that they may turn from darkness to light and from the power of Satan to God, so that they may thus receive forgiveness and release from their sins and a place and portion among those who are consecrated and purified by faith in Me.

John 5:24 (AMP) ²⁴I assure you, most solemnly I tell you, the person whose ears are open to My words [who listens to My message] and believes and trusts in and clings to and relies on Him Who sent Me has (possesses now) eternal life. And he does not come into judgment [does not incur sentence of judgment, will not come under condemnation], but he has already passed over out of death into life.

3) Our mouth/lips – so there is a guard that nothing proceeds out of our mouth but that which is good, edifying, encouraging, glorifying to God and spoken with boldness and power from on high to move our mountains

Proverbs 13:3 (AMP) ³He who guards his mouth keeps his life, but he who opens wide his lips comes to ruin.

Matthew 5:16 (AMP) ¹⁶Let your light so shine before men that they may see your moral excellence and your praiseworthy, noble, and good deeds and recognize and honor and praise and glorify your Father Who is in heaven.

Hebrews 10:25 (AMP) ²⁵Not forsaking or neglecting to assemble together [as believers], as is the habit of some people, but admonishing (warning, urging, and encouraging) one another, and all the more faithfully as you see the day approaching.

Matthew 17:20 (AMP) ²⁰He said to them, Because of the littleness of your faith [that is, your lack of firmly relying trust]. For truly I say to you, if you have faith [that is living] like a grain of mustard seed, you can say to this mountain, Move from here to yonder place, and it will move; and nothing will be impossible to you.

Spiritual Warfare for Kids Beginners I
LESSON 3

ALL AGES TOGETHER – Visual of Roman Armor *(will have two sets for each group)*

Today Breastplate of Righteousness - Visual

Ephesians 6:10-17 (ESV)
The Whole Armor of God
^{10}*Finally, be strong in the Lord and in the strength of his might.* ^{11}*Put on the whole armor of God, that you may be able to stand against the schemes of the devil.* ^{12}*For we do not wrestle against flesh and blood, but against the rulers, against the authorities, against the cosmic powers over this present darkness, against the spiritual forces of evil in the heavenly places.* ^{13}**Therefore take up the whole armor of God, that you may be able to withstand in the evil day, and having done all, to stand firm.** ^{14}**Stand therefore**, *having fastened on the belt of truth, and* **having put on the breastplate of righteousness,** ^{15}*and, as shoes for your feet, having put on the readiness given by the gospel of peace.* ^{16}*In all circumstances take up the shield of faith, with which you can extinguish all the flaming darts of the evil one;* ^{17}*and take the helmet of salvation, and the sword of the Spirit, which is the word of God,*

Pray to equip armor brief

(Divide Groups)

(Words to Song will be posted on wall and sent home for any new kids)

Younger kids/Older kids

Will go over lyrics to third chorus of song.
(This is without music – end of lesson will be music)

Verse Three of Song
NOW THE DEVIL IS A LIAR, DON'T BE FOOLED
STRAP ON YOUR ARMOR WITH THE BELT OF TRUTH
THE DEVIL WILL SHOOT AS WE CONFESS
WE GOT THE BREAST PLATE OF RIGHTEOUSNESS
** WE WILL WE WILL STOMP YOU (3 TIMES)

Review on spiritual battle and helmet of salvation

Open discussion on breastplate of righteousness

- What is righteousness?
- How can we be righteous in God's sight? *(Pick one child each group to come forward to place breastplate on)*
- What does the breastplate cover? *(It covers our heart which is a vital organ)* Explain
- Why would we cover our heart?

Proverbs 22:11 (AMP) [11]He who loves purity and the pure in heart and who is gracious in speech--because of the grace of his lips will he have the king for his friend.

Remember – the helmet protects our mouth that nothing bad comes out and also protects our mind that our thoughts are pure.

(What goes in our mind, goes into our heart and what is in our heart will come out of our mouth)

Matthew 15:18 (AMP) [18]But whatever comes out of the mouth comes from the heart, and this is what makes a man unclean and defiles [him].

Proverbs 4:23 (AMP) [23]Keep and guard your heart with all vigilance and above all that you guard, for out of it flow the springs of life.

ALL AGES TOGETHER

Song – work on and dance steps *(20 minutes)* – send home with any new kids the song/lyrics and all kids the Parent Review for Lesson 3.

PARENTS
(Detailed)
Please review lesson with your child
Spiritual Warfare for Kids Beginners I
LESSON 3 REVIEW

Verse Three of Song
NOW THE DEVIL IS A LIAR, DON'T BE FOOLED
STRAP ON YOUR ARMOR WITH THE BELT OF TRUTH
THE DEVIL WILL SHOOT AS WE CONFESS
WE GOT THE BREAST PLATE OF RIGHTEOUSNESS
** WE WILL WE WILL STOMP YOU (3 TIMES)

Ephesians 6:10-17 (ESV)

The Whole Armor of God

[10] Finally, be strong in the Lord and in the strength of his might. [11] Put on the whole armor of God, that you may be able to stand against the schemes of the devil. [12] For we do not wrestle against flesh and blood, but against the rulers, against the authorities, against the cosmic powers over this present darkness, against the spiritual forces of evil in the heavenly places. **[13] Therefore take up the whole armor of God, that you may be able to withstand in the evil day, and having done all, to stand firm. [14] Stand therefore,** having fastened on the belt of truth, and **having put on the breastplate of righteousness,** [15] and, as shoes for your feet, having put on the readiness given by the gospel of peace. [16] In all circumstances take up the shield of faith, with which you can extinguish all the flaming darts of the evil one; [17] and take the helmet of salvation, and the sword of the Spirit, which is the word of God,

SUMMARY – BREASTPLATE OF RIGHTEOUSNESS ~ PURE HEART

What is righteousness?

Main Focus – Righteousness is doing that which is good and not evil according to truth which is only found in the Word of God. God is Truth.

Impartation – Righteousness is being in right-standing with God, striving to walk the walk and talk the talk. We are covered by grace when we miss it, but it is striving to live a life which is holy and acceptable to God our Father by doing what we know is right and turning from evil.

Note From Author – It is one thing knowing to do what is right and another to actually do what is right. Even in biblical days, we can see that many great men of God missed it and sinned against God. This is one area that satan would love to destroy the Christian. We must understand that this is about what is in our heart. David, a man after God's own heart, committed adultery and also murder. Yet, God loved David. We have to look at this to understand how to be righteous even in times of temptation and missing the mark. Paul tells us in Romans below, that as long as we are in these bodies, we will be at war within to live a life that is righteous.

Romans 7:14-25 (NLT) Struggling with Sin ^{14} So the trouble is not with the law, for it is spiritual and good. The trouble is with me, for I am all too human, a slave to sin. ^{15} I don't really understand myself, for I want to do what is right, but I don't do it. Instead, I do what I hate. ^{16} But if I know that what I am doing is wrong, this shows that I agree that the law is good. ^{17} So I am not the one doing wrong; it is sin living in me that does it. ^{18} And I know that nothing good lives in me, that is, in my sinful nature. I want to do what is right, but I can't. ^{19} I want to do what is good, but I don't. I don't want to do what is wrong, but I do it anyway. ^{20} But if I do what I don't want to do, I am not really the one doing wrong; it is sin living in me that does it. ^{21} I have discovered this principle of life—that when I want to do what is right, I inevitably do what is wrong. ^{22} I love God's law with all my heart. ^{23} But there is another power within me that is at war with my mind. This power makes me a slave to the sin that is still within me. ^{24} Oh, what a miserable person I am! Who will free me from this life that is dominated by sin and death? ^{25} Thank God! The answer is in Jesus Christ our Lord. So you see how it is: In my mind I really want to obey God's law, but because of my sinful nature I am a slave to sin.

Does this give us the right to go ahead and sin? No, it does not. If your heart is right with God, your sin will bother you deeply just as it did David. David cried out to God repeatedly when he missed it. David, the author of the book of Psalm, would write love letters to God. In David's heart, he desired to always do that which was right, but we can see by his life that it was much easier to have that desire to do right than to actually live it. Just as the Scriptures tell us that we will miss it, we have examples throughout the Word of God to show us how even those that seemed to be the greatest men and women, still fell short of walking the walk and talking the talk. You can tell by David's writings that he loved God and desired to do that which was right, but like most of us, David struggled in certain areas where he was weak. We can also tell by Pau's writing in Romans, that he also desired in his heart to live a life of righteousness. However, Paul tells us that the answer is in Jesus Christ. Jesus has already paid the price and overcome this world for us. In John, He had just told His disciples that He was going away, but He let them know that they would have peace through Him along with trials and sorrow. However, we take heart in knowing that He overcame this world for us.

John 16:33 (NLT) [33] *"I have told you all this so that you may have peace in me. Here on earth you will have many trials and sorrows. But take heart, because I have overcome the world."*

In Him, there is nothing we cannot do. If you struggle in certain areas, take heart because your strength to be able to walk through those areas of weakness come from Him. Through Jesus, we are able to make choices based on sound biblical doctrine that will lead us to a life of righteousness.

Philippians 4:13 (NLT) [13] *For I can do everything through Christ, who gives me strength.*

If you have a particular area where you are weak, God still loves you. God desires that you are strengthened in that area where you eventually will be able to stand against that sin and sin no more. We cannot do it in ourselves. In ourselves, we are weak but in Jesus, we are made strong. How do we do this? How do we overcome those areas that weaken us? By spending more time in God's Word. What we must change is our heart so that our desires also change. If your desire was to change where you no longer had the desire to do that particular sin, then you would be strong enough in that area to walk away.

How can we be righteous in God's sight?

Main Focus – It is only through chasing after the One that is righteous that our own righteousness will grow. We become like those where most of our time is spent.

Impartation – Only through Jesus are we righteous. It is not by anything we do, not by works but because Jesus paid that price for us; however, this is not a cop-out! We strive for the mark of the higher calling in and through Christ.

Philippians 3:14 (KJV) [14]I press toward the mark for the prize of the high calling of God in Christ Jesus.

Note From Author – Jesus tells us to ask, seek and knock, and the door will be open. There is a saying that birds of a feather flock together. This means, if we hang out with those that live doing evil, we also will do evil. However, if our associations are with those that are striving for the same mark of the higher calling as we are, then that narrow road which leads to heaven will be easier to travel. However, we must be careful here because it is not about following people. Jesus tells us that many will stand before God as He tells them to depart because He does not know them. God is not talking to those that lived a life denying there was a God, but He is talking to those that were lukewarm. He is talking to those that maybe spent their lives going to church. Salvation is about relationship. God said, *"I never knew you."* A relationship develops between people. It takes at least two people to have a relationship. There are different relationships, but they all mean that you know someone deep enough to have that relationship. There is no relationship with the girl at the grocery store that checks you out each week and speaks to you briefly. You do not really know her intimately. An intimate relationship is one where you are engaged in knowing that person to a deep degree. When we say intimately, that does not mean in a sexual sense. We know someone intimately when we know their heart. This would be like knowing their likes and dislikes, what makes them cry and what makes them happy, etc. You cannot follow the crowd or a particular church just because it seems on the outside that they are really following the bible in its teachings. The problem is that the *"many"* look for a big church that becomes their social outlet. They may connect with others or they may just attend church but outside of church, they never ask, seek or knock. Your relationship with God depends on how well you know Him intimately. You cannot stand before Him and say that you know Him based on what your preacher or anyone else in the church has taught you. They may know Him, but you never did.

It is good to associate with those that are traveling this path, but we won't even know if we are in the right church if we do not seek God ourselves. God desires that you are His child. He desires a relationship with you. He desires to pour revelation into you, and He desires that you hear His voice. Many, many people today claim that they have never heard God's voice. This may be because they do not recognize His voice, but He may actually be speaking to them. In a relationship between two people, there is conversation. A relationship consists of you talking and the other person listening and then the other person talking and you listening or vise versa. Sometimes, we are not listening because we are not asking, seeking or knocking.

If we desire to be righteous in God's sight, we have to know Him. To know Him takes asking. We must first understand what to ask for. When all our asking pertains to something that we want or need Him to do for us, we are missing out on so much more. The first thing we must ask for is the Holy Spirit. Jesus said it was better that He go so that the Holy Spirit would come. The Holy Spirit is referred to as The Helper. He is referred to as The Comforter. Jesus tells us that He, the Holy Spirit, will teach us all things and remind us of all things. We are talking about **ALL** things. If we are to KNOW God, we must have the Holy Spirit living within us which is God's presence in us. This takes asking. We ask and we ask and we ask until we receive the filling of the Holy Spirit. Jesus gives us an example of the lady that repeatedly came before the unjust judge every single day asking and asking for the same thing with the judge sending her away day after day. She did not quit! Remember warriors never quit or give up. Finally, the judge was tired of her persistence and gave her what she wanted. Then Jesus goes on to tell us that this was like His Father. Are we asking but after some time, we give up? You cannot give up. Sometimes God tests us to see just how bad we want something. If you want something bad enough, you will be persistent just like the little old lady.

Luke 18:1-8 (ESV) The Parable of the Persistent Widow 18 And he told them a parable to the effect that they ought always to pray and not lose heart. ² He said, "In a certain city there was a judge who neither feared God nor respected man. ³ And there was a widow in that city who kept coming to him and saying, 'Give me justice against my adversary.' ⁴ For a while he refused, but afterward he said to himself, 'Though I neither fear God nor respect man, ⁵ yet because this widow keeps bothering me, I will give her justice, so that she will not beat me down by her continual coming.'" ⁶ And the Lord said, "Hear what the unrighteous judge says. ⁷ And will not God give justice to his elect, who cry to him day and night? Will he delay long over them? ⁸ I tell you, he will give justice to them speedily. Nevertheless, when the Son of Man comes, will he find faith on earth?"

Sometimes the reason that God does not grant us what we ask for is because we are not seeking. Just asking shows no ambition on your part. The bible says if we don't work we don't eat but really that pertains to anything we desire. If you are not willing to put forth effort, then your asking for the Holy Spirit is just so that you can get what you want when you want it. But, God wants us to have so much more and it takes seeking combined with asking. Seeking means what it says. It's like looking for a treasure. The treasure is there but it depends on how much effort you apply to find that treasure. The treasure we seek for here is God. How do we do this? If you want to find something, you are going to begin by going to the places you think it may be, right? This is why people run to the churches when there is a huge storm in their lives that they cannot cope with. They run to church to hopefully find just a small piece of God in order that He can help them get out of their mess. The sad part is that many times when God comes through and helps them, they stop going to church. Yes, we seek for God in church. We seek for God by associating with those whose lives seem filled with God, but we also must seek for God in His Word. His Word is His love story to you. It is not about making a commitment to read through the bible in one year. Anyone can do that and by the end of the year they may still not know God. Seeking God through His Word is seeking. That means that you pour into His Word. If you were to spend as much time pouring into God's Word as you do pouring into a hobby that you love, you would find Him. We spend countless hours and money pouring into fishing, hunting, shopping, football, making crafts, reading novels that have nothing to do with Jesus, surfing the web, watching television shows that contradict the Word of God and listening to music that defiles God, but we may only dedicate 10 minutes a day to read a small devotion. Or, we may pour countless hours each week watching our children as we teach them how to spend countless hours in dance, pageants, playing on a sports team, etc. It's not that all these things are bad, but if we really want to find God and develop that intimate relationship, it takes seeking deeply.

Seeking doesn't just stop there, we must knock. Knocking involves studying. If you want more of God, in your time of studying His love letter, there will be times that you read something that you want to understand more. This is where all three come into play together – asking, seeking and knocking. We ask, *"God, what does this mean?"* It doesn't stop there, remember. He may not show us that day, but do we stop asking? No, we don't. If you were running for your life and there was a bad guy chasing you, and you saw a house with lights on, what would you do? You would run to that house and begin knocking on the door. You would keep knocking and knocking and asking and asking for someone to open that door, right? God wants us to want Him. He wants us to seek Him. He wants us to continue to pursue Him, and as we are faithful because we do not give up, that door will open. Think of it as your life depending on it. We are running a race and we are being chased. The enemy is right there behind us, chasing us and trying to bring us down. There is one light on and one door that must open to save us. Are you going to first seek finding that door with the light on and then, are you going to knock and knock all the while asking, *"God open the door – I desire to know You – I need You, Holy Spirit – I need Your wisdom God – I need your understanding Lord!"*

So remember, being righteous in the sight of God has nothing to do with doing works to earn your way into heaven. It is all about relationship and seeking God intimately.

Galatians 2:16 (NLT) [16] *"Yet we know that a person is made right with God by faith in Jesus Christ, not by obeying the law. And we have believed in Christ Jesus, so that we might be made right with God because of our faith in Christ, not because we have obeyed the law. For no one will ever be made right with God by obeying the law."*

What does the breastplate cover?

Main Focus – The breastplate of your armor covers your heart which is a vital organ needed for life.

Impartation – Your child learned that the breastplate covers their heart which is an organ that supplies life to their body. The breastplate works hand in hand with the helmet of salvation. Without the helmet, the heart will not survive. The helmet protects and reminds us the importance that what goes into a man is what mirrors their heart. What is in a man's heart is what will come out of their mouth. What proceeds out of your mouth will either produce life or death.

Note From Author – It is important to impart to our children how the whole armor works together for the good. We are all called to be part of the body of Christ to work together for good. We need the mouth, the arms and hands, the legs and feet, and all other parts in order that we are strengthened through Jesus Christ. We will only overcome this world if we are strong. Our strength only comes through Him, but as He equips the body of Christ, we are there to help our brothers and sisters be one with Our Lord.

Why would we cover our heart?

Main Focus – As our heart is the most important vital organ in our natural body in order to have life in the natural, it is also the most important vital organ spiritually and will determine our life after death on this earth.

Impartation – The heart is also the key to salvation. It is with our heart we believe, it is with our heart we love, and it is with our heart we are pure. It is not what goes into a man that is impure but what comes out of a man is what defiles him. We discussed how important it is to stay away from those things which defile us because what we see with our eyes and listen to with our ears goes into our heart and what comes out of our mouth is what is in our heart.

Note From Author – Anytime we have struggles in our lives, it goes back to a heart issue. We are all called for a purpose and throughout our walk in this life, we will face opposition with this world, with material possessions, with our own fleshly desires, with others fighting for our attention, and with the enemy and his tactics. If our heart remains pure and in constant contact with the only One that can give us life and peace and joy on this earth, we should not have struggles. Yes, we will face problems but just as Jesus overcame, we too through Him should overcome. It is not about the storms but about how we face those storms. If you are facing your storms knowing that you are on the winning side, your mentality should say, *"I shall not fear for what can man do to me?"* David faced wars and won. He faced guilt over his choices but still won that battle. He faced the loss of a child but still overcame. He faced rejection and pain from those close to him, but he still continued on the path God chose for him. We too can have the heart of David if we first seek the Kingdom of Heaven because all things will be added to us. We will receive clear direction when faced with opposition by the Lord not by running to others for answers. Seek ye first the kingdom means just that. Either God becomes our

God over all or He is not God at all in our lives. This teaching is to enforce to our children the importance of remaining close to our Lord and Savior in order that our choices in this life are choices which are pure and holy unto our Father and we choose not to listen to the opposition.

Luke 6:45 (ESV) [45]The good person out of the good treasure of his heart produces good, and the evil person out of his evil treasure produces evil, for out of the abundance of the heart his mouth speaks.

Proverbs 22:11 (AMP) [11]He who loves purity and the pure in heart and who is gracious in speech--because of the grace of his lips will he have the king for his friend.

Matthew 15:18 (AMP) [18]But whatever comes out of the mouth comes from the heart, and this is what makes a man unclean and defiles [him].

Proverbs 4:23 (AMP) [23]Keep and guard your heart with all vigilance and above all that you guard, for out of it flow the springs of life.

Spiritual Warfare for Kids Beginners I
LESSON 4

ALL AGES TOGETHER – Visual of Roman Armor *(will have two sets for each group)*

Today Belt of Truth – Visual ~ this is a Roman Belt which covered and protected more than just the waist

Ephesians 6:10-17 (ESV)
The Whole Armor of God
[10]Finally, be strong in the Lord and in the strength of his might. [11] Put on the whole armor of God, that you may be able to stand against the schemes of the devil. [12]For we do not wrestle against flesh and blood, but against the rulers, against the authorities, against the cosmic powers over this present darkness, against the spiritual forces of evil in the heavenly places. **[13]Therefore take up the whole armor of God, that you may be able to withstand in the evil day, and having done all, to stand firm. [14]Stand therefore, having fastened on the belt of truth**, *and having put on the breastplate of righteousness, [15]and, as shoes for your feet, having put on the readiness given by the gospel of peace. [16]In all circumstances take up the shield of faith, with which you can extinguish all the flaming darts of the evil one; [17]and take the helmet of salvation, and the sword of the Spirit, which is the word of God,*

Pray to equip armor brief

(Divide Groups)

(Words to Song will be posted on wall and sent home for any new kids)

Younger kids/Older kids

Will go over lyrics to third chorus of song.
(This is without music – end of lesson will be music)

Verse Three of Song
NOW THE DEVIL IS A LIAR, DON'T BE FOOLED
STRAP ON YOUR ARMOR WITH THE BELT OF TRUTH
THE DEVIL WILL SHOOT AS WE CONFESS
WE GOT THE BREAST PLATE OF RIGHTEOUSNESS
** WE WILL WE WILL STOMP YOU (3 TIMES)

Review on spiritual battle, helmet of salvation and breastplate of righteousness

Open discussion on belt of truth

- What is the belt of truth?
- Why would Paul have used the belt to speak of God's Truth/Word? *(Pick one child each group to come forward to put on belt)*
- What does the belt cover and protect? *(The Roman belt covered and protected vital organs in the midsection of the body. All these organs sustain life but people do undergo surgeries many times to replace these organs in some way; however, many times these replacements alter their lives in drastic ways. When we apply the truth of God's Word to our lives, we are able to see that Jesus died in order to make us complete – that would be made whole, not altered, not with disabilities. Paul teaches that we put on the belt of truth which is to strap it on where it cannot come off – take a leather belt and try to tear it in half with your hands. Belts are made strong to hold items together!)*
- How do we put on the belt of truth?

(Note song says the devil is a liar – satan would like us to listen to him and not to what God's Word says because if we get God's Word down deep in our heart, satan knows

we will become strong and able to walk through our battles and put him under our feet where he belongs)

ALL AGES TOGETHER

Song – work on and dance steps *(20 minutes)* – send home with any new kids the song/lyrics and all kids the Parent Review for Lesson 4.

PARENTS
(Detailed)
Please review lesson with your child
Spiritual Warfare for Kids Beginners I
LESSON 4 REVIEW

Verse Three of Song
NOW THE DEVIL IS A LIAR, DON'T BE FOOLED
STRAP ON YOUR ARMOR WITH THE BELT OF TRUTH
THE DEVIL WILL SHOOT AS WE CONFESS
WE GOT THE BREAST PLATE OF RIGHTEOUSNESS
** WE WILL WE WILL STOMP YOU (3 TIMES)

Ephesians 6:10-17 (ESV)
The Whole Armor of God
[10]Finally, be strong in the Lord and in the strength of his might. [11] Put on the whole armor of God, that you may be able to stand against the schemes of the devil. [12]For we do not wrestle against flesh and blood, but against the rulers, against the authorities, against the cosmic powers over this present darkness, against the spiritual forces of evil in the heavenly places. [13]**<u>Therefore take up the whole armor of God, that you may be able to withstand in the evil day, and having done all, to stand firm. [14]Stand therefore, having fastened on the belt of truth</u>**, and having put on the breastplate of righteousness, [15]and, as shoes for your feet, having put on the readiness given by the gospel of peace. [16]In all circumstances take up the shield of faith, with which you can extinguish all the flaming darts of the evil one; [17]and take the helmet of salvation, and the sword of the Spirit, which is the word of God,

SUMMARY – BELT OF TRUTH ~ GOD'S WORD

What is the belt of truth?

Main Focus – The belt is that one item used to keep something in place.

Impartation – God's Word is Truth. There are no grey areas in this world; it is white or black/ good or evil/ righteousness or sin. Anything contrary to God's Word is not of God!

Note From Author – God is love and God is truth. What we have come to see as truth in this world may not always be truth. God spoke truth in His Word and anything contrary to His Word is not truth. When we apply the Belt of Truth to our lives, it means that we take the Word of God daily and we seek and study to KNOW HIS TRUTH. We will never know truth if we are looking in the wrong places. We have been programmed from day one to see things and believe things according to those that have influenced our lives. As we grow up and get into the public schools and on into college, the brainwashing grows stronger as the enemy uses tactics to influence the minds of our young people to see things according to many well-known philosophers. However, as Christians, we must be that influence that penetrates within our own children to come to know God intimately in order that no tactic designed by our enemy will prosper in their lives. Our children need to be those advocates for Jesus Christ going forward into this dark world bringing truth to the multitudes as they begin to seek for answers that only God can give them.

Why would Paul have used the belt to speak of God's Truth?

Main Focus – The contrast between the belt and the truth used in this illustration focuses on the core existence to our being One with Jesus Christ.

Impartation – A belt is usually used to either secure an outfit, hold something together, or to compliment something. When we use the illustration of a belt to put on God's Word or Truth – we are saying that we are secure in our belief of what the Word of God says. His Truth is what holds us together individually and as the body of Christ. It is His Truth that compliments us or that makes us into something that is extraordinary – perfected into the image of Christ.

Note From Author – When we apply that belt, this means that we have studied to show ourselves approved lacking in nothing. We have made the decision that we choose to follow Jesus Christ and nothing can break away that belt which is securely fastened to our mid-section. The mid-section of our body is where other vital organs are housed and this is considered the core of our existence. The core would be the middle.

What does the belt cover and protect?

Main Focus – The belt covers all the vital organs housed within the mid-section of our bodies in the natural realm. In the spiritual realm, many times our decisions at the last minute are made by a fleeting thought or vision. Sometimes the Holy Spirit will shake us, or we will hear that small quiet voice and make a decision contrary to what we had first planned. Some people call this a gut instinct. They had a feeling that this was what they needed to do or say; this was where they needed to go or what they needed to do. Regardless, that gut feeling involves the mid-section which stirs something up and causes us to feel indifferent. This happens as we pour into God's Word, and it fills our whole being and rises up within us when needed.

Impartation – The Roman belt covered and protected vital organs in the midsection of the body. All these organs sustain life but people many times undergo surgeries to replace different organs in some way to be able to live; however, many times these replacements alter their lives in drastic ways. When we apply the truth of God's Word to our lives, we are able to see that Jesus died in order to make us complete – that would be made whole, not altered, not with disabilities. Paul teaches that we put on the belt of truth which is to strap it on where it cannot come off. Today belts are made in many ways, take a leather belt for instance, leather does not just break. Leather is very strong even when the belt becomes worn; you cannot tear it with your hands. The point it, a belt is made to be strong in order to secure what it is being used for. However, the Roman belt was made of bronze plates and leather. It was the foundation which helped support the breastplate and kept it secure along with holding all the weapons. As the belt of truth, this is a parallel to Jesus being our solid foundation.

Note From Author – In the natural, we take care to keep the organs in our mid-section working properly by supplying needed nutrients in order that everything flows smoothly throughout our being. In the spiritual realm, we understand that we face battles everyday as our enemy behind the scene tries to destroy our faith, our determination, our energy, our resources, our families, etc. In knowing this area must be covered to overcome the tactics of our enemy, our belts must stay secured and that can only happen as we fill our lives with His Word. We must study to show ourselves approved and ready for the battle at hand daily.

How do we put the belt of truth on?

Main Focus – We must understand that our choices daily affect whether we walk into battle with our Belt of Truth on or off.

Impartation – We fasten it on. When we put any belt on, we have to put it on and fasten it. We make that choice to put on the truth and walk with Christ as our foundation. We make the choice to not listen to lies but to stand firmly fixed on what God's Word says.

Note From Author – Daily, the enemy will place obstacles in our paths that will tempt us to loosen our belt or compromise. Our decisions determine if we are prepared for battle. Our choices will reflect our lives being filled with either peace or turmoil – joy or unhappiness. When you find yourself in a situation where there is no peace, look back to the place where you made the choice to loosen your belt. Once it becomes loose, it will fall off. We must daily seek God and daily, study His Word. Then and only then, will we be strengthened enough to overcome all temptations. Cry out to the Lord our God when faced with turmoil that He forgives and sets you back on the path from which you turned. By grace you are saved and His mercy will forgive your wrong choices, but we must teach our children that peace does come to all those that follow close in His footsteps. Even in the midst of a battle we can conquer.

Note the song says the devil is a liar – satan would like us to listen to him and not to what God's Word says because if we get God's Word down deep in our heart, satan knows we will become strong and able to walk through our battles and put him under our feet where he belongs.

SPIRITUAL WARFARE FOR KIDS BEGINNERS II

Spiritual Warfare for Kids Beginners II
LESSON 1

ALL AGES TOGETHER – Visual of Roman Armor *(two sets for each group)*

Today – Review over SWKBI ~ Visual of Armor Covered

Ephesians 6:10-17 (ESV)
The Whole Armor of God
[10]Finally, be strong in the Lord and in the strength of his might. [11] Put on the whole armor of God, that you may be able to stand against the schemes of the devil. [12]For we do not wrestle against flesh and blood, but against the rulers, against the authorities, against the cosmic powers over this present darkness, against the spiritual forces of evil in the heavenly places. **[13]Therefore take up the whole armor of God, that you may be able to withstand in the evil day, and having done all, to stand firm. [14]Stand therefore, having fastened on the belt of truth, and having put on the breastplate of righteousness,** *[15]and, as shoes for your feet, having put on the readiness given by the gospel of peace. [16]In all circumstances take up the shield of faith, with which you can extinguish all the flaming darts of the evil one;* **[17]and take the helmet of salvation**, *and the sword of the Spirit, which is the word of God,*

Pray to equip armor brief

(Divide Groups)

(Words to Song will be posted on wall)

Younger kids/Older kids

Will go over lyrics to first, second, and third chorus of song.

(This is without music – end of lesson will be music)

MOMMA ALWAYS TOLD ME TO PRAY REAL HARD
DO THE RIGHT THING AND LIVE FOR GOD
I'M A WARRIOR FOR LIFE – FOR JESUS CHRIST
FIGHTING THE DEVIL WITH ALL MY MIGHT
** WE WILL WE WILL STOMP YOU

NOW LISTEN REAL CLOSE TO WHAT I SAY
WALK THRU YOUR BATTLES WITH YOUR SHIELD OF FAITH
GOD IS FOREVER AND I'M HIS CREATION
RUN THIS RACE WITH YOUR HELMET OF SALVATION
** WE WILL WE WILL STOMP YOU

NOW THE DEVIL IS A LIAR, DON'T BE FOOLED
STRAP ON YOUR ARMOR WITH THE BELT OF TRUTH
THE DEVIL WILL SHOOT AS WE CONFESS
WE GOT THE BREAST PLATE OF RIGHTEOUSNESS
** WE WILL WE WILL STOMP YOU

Review on spiritual battle, helmet of salvation, breastplate of righteousness & belt of truth

Open discussion/Question and Answers

- Review topics from SWKBI before proceeding. *(Children must have gone through SWKBI in order to attend SWKBII)*

ALL AGES TOGETHER

Song – work on and dance steps *(20 minutes)* – there will be review sheets, song/lyrics for any who need them; otherwise, there is no Parents Review sheet for SWKBII-Lesson 1.

Spiritual Warfare for Kids Beginners II
LESSON 2

ALL AGES TOGETHER – Visual of Roman Armor *(two sets for each group)*

Today Gospel Shoes – Visual

Ephesians 6:10-17 (ESV)
The Whole Armor of God
¹⁰Finally, be strong in the Lord and in the strength of his might. ¹¹ Put on the whole armor of God, that you may be able to stand against the schemes of the devil. ¹²For we do not wrestle against flesh and blood, but against the rulers, against the authorities, against the cosmic powers over this present darkness, against the spiritual forces of evil in the heavenly places. **¹³Therefore take up the whole armor of God, that you may be able to withstand in the evil day, and having done all, to stand firm. ¹⁴Stand therefore**, *having fastened on the belt of truth, and having put on the breastplate of righteousness,* **¹⁵and, as shoes for your feet, having put on the readiness given by the gospel of peace.** *¹⁶In all circumstances take up the shield of faith, with which you can extinguish all the flaming darts of the evil one; ¹⁷and take the helmet of salvation, and the sword of the Spirit, which is the word of God,*

Pray to equip armor brief

(Divide Groups)

(Words to Song will be posted on wall)

Younger kids/Older kids

Will go over lyrics to the fourth chorus of song.
(This is without music – end of lesson will be music)

Verse Four of Song
SATAN ATTACKS KNOWING HE'S HELL BOUND
WITH MY SWORD OF THE SPIRIT I WILL BRING HIM DOWN
GOT GOD ON MY SIDE AND I CAN'T LOSE
STOMPIN THE DEVIL WITH MY GOSPEL SHOES
** WE WILL WE WILL STOMP YOU (3 TIMES)

Open discussion on gospel shoes

- What are gospel shoes?
- Why does God expect us to prepare ourselves? *(Pick one child each group to come forward to place shoes on)*
- What do our shoes protect?
- How do we prepare ourselves for this calling?
- The song says that we stomp the devil with our gospel shoes, how does putting on our gospel shoes stomp the devil?

ALL AGES TOGETHER

Song – work on and dance steps *(20 minutes)* – send home with all children the Parent Review for Lesson 2.

PARENTS
(Detailed)
Spiritual Warfare for Kids Beginners II
LESSON 2 REVIEW

Verse Four of Song
SATAN ATTACKS KNOWING HE'S HELL BOUND
WITH MY SWORD OF THE SPIRIT I WILL BRING HIM DOWN
GOT GOD ON MY SIDE AND I CAN'T LOSE
STOMPIN THE DEVIL WITH MY GOSPEL SHOES
*** WE WILL WE WILL STOMP YOU (3 TIMES)*

Ephesians 6:10-17 (ESV)
The Whole Armor of God
[10]Finally, be strong in the Lord and in the strength of his might. [11] Put on the whole armor of God, that you may be able to stand against the schemes of the devil. [12]For we do not wrestle against flesh and blood, but against the rulers, against the authorities, against the cosmic powers over this present darkness, against the spiritual forces of evil in the heavenly places. <u>**[13]Therefore take up the whole armor of God, that you may be able to withstand in the evil day, and having done all, to stand firm.** *[14]***Stand therefore**</u>, *having fastened on the belt of truth, and having put on the breastplate of righteousness,* <u>**[15]and, as shoes for your feet, having put on the readiness given by the gospel of peace.**</u> *[16]In all circumstances take up the shield of faith, with which you can extinguish all the flaming darts of the evil one; [17]and take the helmet of salvation, and the sword of the Spirit, which is the word of God,*

SUMMARY – GOSPEL SHOES

What are gospel shoes?

Main Focus – As a Christian, you have made the choice to follow Jesus and that is following in His footsteps. Our gospel shoes are placed upon our feet to carry us into the battle field. Being the disciples we were called to be, we go forth to share the same message that Jesus shared.

Impartation – In verse 15 of Ephesians, it talks about getting your shoes ready, your feet prepared to put on your gospel shoes. In the amplified translation, it says to face the enemy and to do so by being prepared which only happens through the good news, which is God's Word, the Gospel of Peace. When we put on our shoes, what we are saying is that we are ready to go forth and share Jesus with the world. We come to that place where we are not ashamed of what we believe and what we stand for. This is affirmation of our faith in Christ and at this place is where we will face the enemy, but your children are learning that their armor will prepare them for every encounter.

Note From Author – We are all called but not all chosen. Your choices in this life will determine if you are chosen. If an actor or actress goes forth to try out in hopes of being chosen for a particular character in a movie, all are called that may have what it takes to play that role but not all are chosen. All go forth to rehearse for that screen play but the one chosen would be the one that best performs. The one chosen will be the one that gives it all they have and were meant for that particular character based on their own personalities. In this one life that you have been given, the Lord has equipped you with the Word of God to prepare you to be one of His chosen. There are multitudes of personalities needed for all the different characters that will play a role in bringing the gospel to this world. The storms you have encountered in your life have shaped your character to make it unique for the calling that God has placed upon your life, but it takes you stepping out and giving it all you have in order to be chosen. Your life is your own movie but whether you make the choice to go to work each day to fulfill what you were called to do will depend totally on what is in your heart. The problem in this world is the *"many"* will not be chosen because the desires are not within most Christians to lay their own lives at the Cross and meet Jesus halfway. The *"many"* choose a life in this world with the desires to indulge in the riches that we see with our natural eyes and not with our spiritual eyes. To be chosen, will literally take dying to your own agenda and desires and then applying those gospel shoes to your life, so that you are ever ready to present the gospel to those that God sends your way.

Ephesians 6:15 (AMP) ¹⁵And having shod your feet in preparation [to face the enemy with the firm-footed stability, the promptness, and the readiness produced by the good news] of the Gospel of peace.

Once the decision is made and your will lines up with the Father, your shoes must be on so that you are ready to face the enemy and all that satan may bring your way in order to bring you down. However, as long as you go forth with your full armor on, satan will be a defeated foe. In Psalms it says that even though you may stumble, you will not fall. God takes care of those that are His!

*Psalm 37:23-24 (NLT) [23] The L*ORD *directs the steps of the godly. He delights in every detail of their lives. [24] Though they stumble, they will never fall, for the L*ORD *holds them by the hand*

Why does God expect us to prepare ourselves?

Main Focus – We must be prepared to gain ground and win battles. Without preparation, we are open to being destroyed.

Impartation – We are expected as Christians to share the gospel. This is for everyone who claims to be a Child of God. We do not sit on the sidelines and play church. We realize there is a real battle out there, and we are to be prepared with our full armor in order to bring down the enemy and everything that exalts itself against the knowledge of Christ.

Mark 16:15 (KJV) ⁱ⁵And he said unto them, Go ye into all the world, and preach the gospel to every creature.

John 14:23 (AMP) ²³Jesus answered, If a person [really] loves Me, he will keep My word [obey My teaching]; and My Father will love him, and We will come to him and make Our home (abode, special dwelling place) with him.

Note From Author - In a natural war, if you are not prepared to face the enemy in the battle field, you will fall but so will those that you are leading if you are of high rank. In a spiritual war, when you travel the wrong path, you are also leading your family and friends into an ambush which ultimately brings destruction and a spiritual death. To go further and look at the larger puzzle, besides those you are close to, there are many others in this world that your specific character, along with the storms you have walked through and gained wisdom, could drastically and radically impact those lives as well. However, when we choose rather a life of luxury and living for the indulgences of this world, we teach those around us to do the same.

Hebrews 11:24-27 (NLT) ²⁴ It was by faith that Moses, when he grew up, refused to be called the son of Pharaoh's daughter. ²⁵ He chose to share the oppression of God's people instead of enjoying the fleeting pleasures of sin. ²⁶ He thought it was better to suffer for the sake of Christ than to own the treasures of Egypt, for he was looking ahead to his great reward. ²⁷ It was by faith that

Moses left the land of Egypt, not fearing the king's anger. He kept right on going because he kept his eyes on the one who is invisible.

Moses knew that the things which cannot be seen far outweighed those things which can be seen. In America, we all fall into the trap and tactics set out by the enemy to gain our attentions. We have to learn balance in order to teach our children that the greatest riches by far are those things which cannot be seen.

2 Corinthians 10:4-5 (KJV) [4](For the weapons of our warfare are not carnal, but mighty through God to the pulling down of strong holds;) [5]Casting down imaginations, and every high thing that exalteth itself against the knowledge of God, and bringing into captivity every thought to the obedience of Christ;

What do our shoes protect?

Main Focus – Our gospel shoes inure us that the path we will choose in this life will be that road which leads us to Our Savior. One pathway leads to life while the other leads to death. Without the gospel shoes on, there is no assurance that you are traveling the right path.

Impartation – Our shoes protect our feet and our feet carry us where we are going. When we begin preparing ourselves to share Jesus by studying to show ourselves approved, God will begin to put that unction within us to go and share. The gospel will rise up in us everywhere we go. God's Word should be a lamp unto our feet and a light unto our path. Your child is learning that being prepared means to make those choices to walk down the path which is light and avoid the dark. The dark areas many times are traps or tactics set out by our enemy.

Psalm 119:105 (KJV) [105]Thy word is a lamp unto my feet, and a light unto my path.

Note From Author – We will all choose one pathway in this life. As we travel down our weary roads, many times we come to a fork in the road. God has placed many forks along the roads we are traveling, but the enemy also has forks in the road. When we are traveling down the pathway which leads to heaven, you can bet there are traps set out on that narrow path with an alternate road to entice us. Look at it from this standpoint, while traveling down the narrow road following in the footsteps of Jesus, we become weary and need rest. All of a sudden, we take time out to relax and we remove our gospel shoes to rest our feet. While taking time out sitting on the side of the road, we look off into the distance. There is a billboard that has an arrow with an alternate path. The billboard has your weakness printed all over it showing much gratification and indulgence into this world. *"Turn this way,"* the billboard says, *"here is your dream for today. Take time out to enjoy and be filled with much peace and happiness, after all, a little fun for one day doesn't hurt anyone but you must not put back on those gospel shoes because your fun will be limited."*

Here's what happens, we buy into a lie from the enemy, and we step out making the wrong choice. We make the choice to take a detour from the narrow path that God chose for us. The gospel shoes automatically come off because when we make the choice to go our own way and not the path God chose, *"My will Father and not Your will,"* we are separated from His best. We begin to travel the alternate pathway, and it all seems good for the time being. But, then we realize that we are facing adversity and the joy and peace seem to be gone. We begin to cry out to God once again and like a loving Father, as we are sitting on the side of the alternate roadway broken, we look up and there is another fork in the road. This time it is to bring us back to the narrow road which leads to heaven.

Daily, you will face trials and tests that are designed to strengthen you by God and other storms that are designed by our enemy to bring you down. It is imperative that our gospel shoes remain intact on our feet so that our choices lead and keep us on one pathway, the only pathway that keeps us in constant peace even when faced with adversity!

For our children, that billboard may be something as simple as choosing to spend countless hours in front of the television instead of developing relationships. Following the wrong pathway has nothing to do with making the choice to follow what we look at as sin. Sin can also be turning from opportunities to witness Jesus because we are too busy entertaining our flesh. It may be making the choice to break one of the 10 commandments or simply choosing a self-centered pathway that is all about doing what we desire for that day instead of listening to the Holy Spirit lead our path for a particular situation. Relationships are far greater than anything that can occupy your time. Teaching our children that the greatest treasures in this world are people and not things go a long way with developing their character to be those Disciples for Jesus Christ.

How do we prepare ourselves for this calling?

Main Focus – We begin by gaining knowledge.

Impartation – We study and learn of God daily. We do not let the Word of God depart from us, but we keep it deep in our heart so that our feet do not wander from the light and then we make those choices to go forth to share Jesus boldly and unashamed.

Romans 10:11 (KJV) ¹¹For the scripture saith, Whosoever believeth on him shall not be ashamed.

Note From Author – If we go to college to gain knowledge in a certain field of study, we will spend several years reading and listening to instructors so that we can show ourselves approved. If we are not approved, we gain no degree.

2 Timothy 2:15 (KJV) ¹⁵Study to shew thyself approved unto God, a workman that needeth not to be ashamed, rightly dividing the word of truth.

If you desire to be a doctor, you will spend many years studying before you ever step out to practice in that field. Once you have gained the knowledge, which is gained by reading and studying, the next step is to gain wisdom. Wisdom comes with time. A doctor does not go to college, get his doctorate degree and open up an office to begin his practice as a doctor when he has had no on-hand training. We do not want a doctor diagnosing our illnesses or a surgeon cutting on us, if they have had no hands-on practice under a physician or surgeon. Book knowledge is not enough to begin your practice, the same with being a warrior in God' army. We do not want to be on the battlefield alone, and we certainly do not want rookies with no training fighting alongside of us. In fact, the Word of God tells us that we perish because of lack of knowledge.

Hosea 4:6 (ESV) ⁶My people are destroyed for lack of knowledge; because you have rejected knowledge,

The first part of preparation begins with gaining the knowledge, and as you gain knowledge, by reading and studying and seeking God, the day will come when God opens a door for you to begin gaining wisdom.

Wisdom is acquired as you step out into the battlefield. A doctor's wisdom is acquired by hands on training once he has come to the place to work up under a licensed doctor. Hands on gains wisdom, you learn by doing. This is where we are called to *"go!"* When we go, we are stepping out into the battlefield at this point. This is when all hell breaks loose. This is the place where you get to practice your faith. Without faith, we are not pleasing to God.

Hebrews 11:6 (ESV) ⁶And without faith it is impossible to please him, for whoever would draw near to God must believe that he exists and that he rewards those who seek him.

Faith says, *"No matter how hard the storms get, I will not quit."* A true Disciple of Jesus Christ will continue to tread on and trust in God. In the battlefield, your storms will be fierce because you are in training. In a real boot camp, they are preparing soldiers for the real battlefield so they simulate what that may be like. A real boot camp is designed to be as fierce as they can make it because they know the actual battle will be far worse than you can imagine. A Disciple for Jesus Christ is one that is willing to die for Christ. A Disciple for Jesus Christ says, *"Lord, I love you no matter what!"* The good news is that as you are in training to gain wisdom, you are going to gain wisdom. Having wisdom is far better than being ignorant while trying to live a life with Jesus Christ as you continue to remain a rookie all the while, never growing up and never gaining the true riches of the gospel. There is so much more if we are willing to keep those gospel shoes on and tread through the waters and through the fires knowing that Our God will never leave nor forsake us. You are never alone in your battlefield! There may be time when you feel forsaken, but be of good cheer knowing you will make it through unharmed and unscathed. You are a child of the most-high God, and if He has you in a place of battle, He is not done with you yet. There is so much more!

Deuteronomy 31:6 (ESV) ⁶"Be strong and courageous. Do not fear or be in dread of them, for it is the L<small>ORD</small> your God who goes with you. He will not leave you or forsake you."

The last step you should strive for is the understanding. Many times when faced with a storm, we cry out, *"Why God, why do I have to go through this? Your Word says that you will never give me more than I can handle."*

1 Corinthians 10:13 (NLT) ¹³ The temptations in your life are no different from what others experience. And God is faithful. He will not allow the temptation to be more than you can stand. When you are tempted, he will show you a way out so that you can endure.

Sometimes, we need the understanding, and sometimes, we just need to trust. Many times God will give us the understanding for a particular storm but sometimes, it may be years before we are actually able to look back and gain the understanding of why we had to endure and go through that storm. There is always a reason, but we need to understand that God's plan is far greater than any plan we may have had. This is where trust comes in. *"God, I may not understand but I trust that You have a perfect plan."* Lauren Daigle, a Christian artist, sings a song called, *"Trust In You."* The song says, *"When You don't move the mountains I'm needing you to move, when you don't part the waters I wish I could walk through, when you don't give the answers as I cry out to You, I will trust in You."*[3]

Jesus had to trust that God's plan was greater when He went and prayed in the Garden of Gethsemane. *"Not my will Lord but Your will be done!"* This has to be our prayer as a soldier in the Army of God. We may not understand today, but tomorrow we may be given that understanding. Understanding will only come as we are faithful which takes letting go and just trusting in Him. Our lives are never a mistake. We find ourselves in certain situations, but God already knew what choice we would have made to put us where we are. God allowed for our sins and designed a perfect plan based on our choices but at some point, we have to choose that narrow pathway to begin our travels into a life as a true Disciple of Jesus Christ. This is a journey and one that leads to great knowledge, wisdom and understanding.

The song says that we stomp the devil with our gospel shoes, how does putting on our gospel shoes stomp the devil?

Main Focus – Saying yes to God and no to all else, puts us in the same place Jesus was when He defeated satan.

Impartation – According to Scripture, we have been given the authority to trample upon anything the enemy possesses. Our gospel shoes are prepared with the wisdom and knowledge of Christ, and we use that tool to put satan under our feet where he belongs.

Note From Author – This goes back to choices once again. Jesus had to make the choice to die to self. *"Father, not My will be done but Your will."* We too must make that choice every day. As Jesus faced satan in the desert, there were many different paths to choose as satan used various tactics to entice Jesus in the flesh. As the Son of God, Jesus was still a man and still lived in an earthly body which felt pain, rejection, torment, loneliness, love, etc. Jesus felt emotions just as we feel them. He learned to love as He walked among the people and understood what they faced daily. Jesus was saddened when Lazarus died. Even though He brought Him back to life, He felt the pain of loss. Jesus was saddened when He heard that John the Baptist had been beheaded. He knew He would see him again, but He felt the loss. In the earthly body, He hurt for mankind in the same way that we do. This is why the bible tells us that God desires that none should perish. God wants all of us to be comforted by the Holy Spirit. He desires that all of us find the truth. He desires that all of us grow spiritually so that we can face the battles and triumph over the enemy by having the eyes to see and the ears to hear truth. Without truth, there is no knowledge and we perish. Jesus had truth in Him – He was God and He was Truth. His eyes and ears could see in the spiritual realm but ours can also if we want it bad enough. We have everything it takes to walk in victory. He came to give life and give it in abundance. We will have trouble but we can overcome just as He did in the desert. Knowing truth, we will know what road to travel and when to say no to the forks in the road that lead away from God. Saying *"No"* to the enemy says *"Yes"* to God and our shoes remain on keeping the enemy under our feet just as Jesus did in the desert.

Luke 10:19 (AMP) ¹⁹Behold! I have given you authority and power to trample upon serpents and scorpions, and [physical and mental strength and ability] over all the power that the enemy [possesses]; and nothing shall in any way harm you.

Spiritual Warfare for Kids Beginners II
LESSON 3

ALL AGES TOGETHER – Visual of Roman Armor *(two sets for each group)*

Today Shield of Faith – Visual

Ephesians 6:10-17 (ESV)
The Whole Armor of God
¹⁰Finally, be strong in the Lord and in the strength of his might. ¹¹ Put on the whole armor of God, that you may be able to stand against the schemes of the devil. **¹²For we do not wrestle against flesh and blood, but against the rulers, against the authorities, against the cosmic powers over this present darkness, against the spiritual forces of evil in the heavenly places. ¹³Therefore take up the whole armor of God, that you may be able to withstand in the evil day, and having done all, to stand firm.** ¹⁴Stand therefore, having fastened on the belt of truth, and having put on the breastplate of righteousness, ¹⁵and, as shoes for your feet, having put on the readiness given by the gospel of peace. **¹⁶In all circumstances take up the shield of faith, with which you can extinguish all the flaming darts of the evil one;** ¹⁷and take the helmet of salvation, and the sword of the Spirit, which is the word of God,

Pray to equip armor brief

(Divide Groups)

(Words to Song will be posted on wall)

Younger kids/Older kids

Will go over lyrics to the second chorus of song.
(This is without music – end of lesson will be music)

Verse Two of Song
NOW LISTEN REAL CLOSE TO WHAT I SAY
WALK THRU YOUR BATTLES WITH YOUR SHIELD OF FAITH
GOD IS FOREVER AND I'M HIS CREATION
RUN THIS RACE WITH YOUR HELMET OF SALVATION
** WE WILL WE WILL STOMP YOU (3 TIMES)

Review gospel shoes

Open discussion on shield of faith

- What is faith?
- Why do we have to have faith? *(Pick one child each group to come forward and hold the shield of faith – and   explain that the Roman shield in biblical days covered the whole body and was curved)*
- What does the shield protect? *(And, why was it curved)*
- How can we exercise our faith?

ALL AGES TOGETHER

Song – work on and dance steps *(20 minutes)* – send home with all children the Parent Review for Lesson 3.

PARENTS
(Detailed)
Spiritual Warfare for Kids Beginners II
LESSON 3 REVIEW

Verse Two of Song
NOW LISTEN REAL CLOSE TO WHAT I SAY
WALK THRU YOUR BATTLES WITH YOUR SHIELD OF FAITH
GOD IS FOREVER AND I'M HIS CREATION
RUN THIS RACE WITH YOUR HELMET OF SALVATION
*** WE WILL WE WILL STOMP YOU (3 TIMES)*

Ephesians 6:10-17 (ESV)
The Whole Armor of God
[10] Finally, be strong in the Lord and in the strength of his might. [11] Put on the whole armor of God, that you may be able to stand against the schemes of the devil. **[12] For we do not wrestle against flesh and blood, but against the rulers, against the authorities, against the cosmic powers over this present darkness, against the spiritual forces of evil in the heavenly places. [13] Therefore take up the whole armor of God, that you may be able to withstand in the evil day, and having done all, to stand firm.** [14] Stand therefore, having fastened on the belt of truth, and having put on the breastplate of righteousness, [15] and, as shoes for your feet, having put on the readiness given by the gospel of peace. **[16] In all circumstances take up the shield of faith, with which you can extinguish all the flaming darts of the evil one;** [17] and take the helmet of salvation, and the sword of the Spirit, which is the word of God,

SUMMARY – SHEILD OF FAITH

What is faith?

Main Focus – Faith believes for the impossible. To God, nothing is impossible.

Impartation – Faith is when you believe those things that are not as though they were according to Hebrews.

Hebrews 11:1-5 (NLT) Great Examples of Faith 11 Faith is the confidence that what we hope for will actually happen; it gives us assurance about things we cannot see. ² Through their faith, the people in days of old earned a good reputation. ³ By faith we understand that the entire universe was formed at God's command, that what we now see did not come from anything that can be seen. ⁴ It was by faith that Abel brought a more acceptable offering to God than Cain did. Abel's offering gave evidence that he was a righteous man, and God showed his approval of his gifts. Although Abel is long dead, he still speaks to us by his example of faith. ⁵ It was by faith that Enoch was taken up to heaven without dying—"he disappeared, because God took him." For before he was taken up, he was known as a person who pleased God.

Note From Author – In other words, by faith we believe that God has healed us even though the symptoms may say we are not healed. We do not go by what we feel but what we know to be true according to the Word of God. An example – Doctors said I could never carry a child to full term but I received a *Rhema* Word from God that said I could. My faith was then tested when I became pregnant and began to lose that baby. Doctors said the baby would not live but God told me different. I placed my faith in God and did according to what He told me to do and the baby lived. *(There are many examples you can use with your child – but it is when your faith is tested and you make the decision to go with what the Word says and not the world, this is when you will receive your miracle according to God's Word)*

Why do we have to have faith?

Main Focus – Without faith we are not pleasing to God.

Hebrews 11:6 (NLT) ⁶And it is impossible to please God without faith. Anyone who wants to come to him must believe that God exists and that he rewards those who sincerely seek him.

Impartation – We all have a measure of faith and it is by faith that we believe there is a God, that Jesus is the Son of God, etc. In order to be a warrior, we must learn to exercise our faith so that it increases. The bible talks about moving mountains and Jesus tells His disciples, *"Oh ye of little faith."* We cannot move mountains or live a life of faith to please God without making changes in order that our faith grows to greater depths.

Matthew 8:26 (KJV) ²⁶And he saith unto them, Why are ye fearful, O ye of little faith? Then he arose, and rebuked the winds and the sea; and there was a great calm.

Note From Author – Your faith will only grow as you are in the battlefield facing difficulties. We must stop complaining when we find ourselves in storms. We are so used to crying out to God to deliver us from our storms. Most of our storms today are the result of God doing a work in us. He desires that we rise up to be warriors ready to face anything and ready to die for the cause if need be. In New Testament times, the disciples died to self and gave all they had for the gospels in order to get the Word out to the multitudes that Jesus died and rose again to give us life. Our life is not our own. Our life belongs to Him if you call yourselves a Christian. We die at the Cross and meet Christ and then we study to gain knowledge in order to go forth to spread the truth. Faith trusts in God. Facing situations in our lives, your faith must say, *"Lord, I do not understand why I am facing this, but I know your plan is greater than my plan, and I pray that You teach me what it is I am to learn."* Any great man or woman of God that has a powerful anointed message will tell you that they have walked through fierce storms in their life to be where they are with God. The more you have endured, the greater your ministry will be. Your situations will touch the lives of all those that may be facing similar difficulties because you are there to tell them, *"I have been in your shoes."* You are there to show them how you walked through that storm. The wisdom that you gained by remaining faithful and trusting in God through your storm, showed Him that you trusted that His plan was better than any choice you could have made.

Being a warrior in God's army is a great honor. A war is not always a bad thing when the result of that war produces something great. America won its independence and freedom to be able to worship our God and break away from the tyranny of Great Britian, but it took fighting for those rights. The price paid in any war results in many lives lost. All is good when we realize that it is not about this life but the life to come. The disciples understood this and gave it everything. Even though they lost their natural life, they gained a life eternal with their Lord Jesus Christ. The result of their faithfulness was that the message of Jesus Christ still lives today.

We are facing a time in America, where we are losing ground and the enemy is gaining the minds of the majority that our country is becoming one where the Christians are the minority. There are few Christians willing to give it all they have knowing it may cost them everything, but if we do not instill in our children the importance of freedom to worship Our God, America will surely fall. This country was founded on Christian principles and turning from this will result in judgment from Our Father upon this country. We must make a decision in this life and teach our children, if the disciples in the days of Jesus were willing to die for truth, are our lives any greater that we should not be willing to do the same so that the message continues in America until Jesus returns?

John 13:37 (NLV) ³⁷ Peter said to Jesus, "Why can I not follow You now? I will die for You."

Even though, the story goes that Peter denied Jesus three times, those words became truth when eventually, Peter was crucified. As Peter grew with the Holy Spirit, He chose the path to give it all because he knew the life to come was far greater than anything on this earth.

Hebrews 11:6 (KJV) ⁶But without faith it is impossible to please him: for he that cometh to God must believe that he is, and that he is a rewarder of them that diligently seek him.

Matthew 17:20 (AMP) ²⁰He said to them, Because of the littleness of your faith [that is, your lack of firmly relying trust]. For truly I say to you, if you have faith [that is living] like a grain of mustard seed, you can say to this mountain, Move from here to yonder place, and it will move; and nothing will be impossible to you.

Our faith should say, "Lord, whatever plan you have for my life, let it be one that impacts lives in this *world and let my life be an example which gives glory unto You."*

What does the shield protect?

Main Focus – Full of faith, there is a shield around you which keeps you safe as you go forth in the calling placed upon your life.

Impartation – The Roman Shield was long and curved. It covered the whole body and was curved to protect the sides as well. It was made of strong wood because during war when a fiery dart hit the shield, it would go into the wood enough that it put the fire out. The darts in those days were lit on fire and when they hit something, they would explode unless they were extinguished. Paul used this as a parallel to show us that our shield which is our faith is our defensive weapon. If you can understand a card game and how one opponent may bluff the other opponent, it is by this bluff that many times a card game is actually won. Our faith is walking this walk with Christ as well as talking it. If we do not learn how to fight the enemy by our words, we will always feel defeated. When we raise our shield, we are actually increasing our faith by walking the walk and talking the talk.

Note From Author – The shield of faith is the armor that we learn to use after we have secured our gospel shoes on and have gone into the battlefield. It looks something like this, according to Scripture – we first apply the Belt of Truth. Without having God's Word grounded in us, there is NO knowledge. Your knowledge gained in this world will only bring you defeat when up against our enemy. In gaining knowledge through the Word of God, it goes hand in hand with the Breastplate of Righteousness. However, even if we have acquired a lot of knowledge in the Word of God there still may be some areas that God needs to deal with in each of our lives personally. Whatever hurts and pains you have endured prior to knowing Jesus, you have stored them in your heart. Once you are able to trust God because you have come to know Him by seeking Him in His Word, He can then begin to open up your heart to heal any pain where those walls that you have built around you can be broken down to learn to trust whole heartedly. Your heart, needing the Breastplate of Righteousness, must first open up to trust and love like Jesus. This takes allowing the Holy Spirit to come into our lives and clean house. He removes the junk and fills us with His presence. You are ready for battle at this point. Here come the gospel shoes and the wisdom. As you are in the battlefield, there are angels encamped around you and the Holy Spirit walking with you.

However, much of this battle has to do with letting go of you and trusting Him. This is why we remain in our storms for long periods of time. He is preparing you. He gives us tools for fighting in the battlefield. The first tool is the Shield of Faith. As we discussed, the storms grow your faith. However, sometimes the storms can really be fierce and sometimes the storms are God allowing satan to bring us to the end of ourselves. Job had one such storm. God must know what we are made of before we can graduate through boot camp. Now we have the Shield of Faith but we must learn how to use it. We must learn what it is for and how it will protect us. The first thing to know is that the Shield of Faith in battle is there to cover us completely.

Many people teach this concept. There is an umbrella of protection over us where God keeps us safe as long as we remain under that protection. When we make choices that conflict with His will, we step out from under that umbrella and are open to the attacks of satan. However, we are going to choose rather to look at this in a biblical sense. There is a Shield of Protection which was used by the Romans in biblical days to protect their whole body dependent on where it was held. The shield in those days completely covered the entire body held in the front along with the sides, but when in battle, you had to hold the shield and fight from one side or the other. The shield basically kept darts or fiery darts from being shot directly into your body as long as the shield was held up to cover you. Paul used this to emphasize what our spiritual shield looks like. In the battle, we cannot just stand there trying to hide behind this shield. We trust God in the battle, and we are constantly on guard looking for any tactics of the enemy in order that we are able to keep those fiery darts from penetrating into any parts of our body. Enticements to the eyes, enticements to the ears, enticements to our heart, are all tactics. We are brought down by the enemy when we become complacent and let our guard down. The shield is your guard. Angels are there to protect you and the Holy Spirit is there to fight with you. God has given us many things to win our battles, but He desires that we train to become warriors and in doing so, we go into boot camp and come out true Disciples for Jesus Christ willing to lay our own lives at the Cross.

How can we increase our faith?

Main Focus – We go forth into the battlegrounds and use what has been given to us.

Impartation – Once again, faith grows as you use it. Example: We lose what we do not use. If we stopped walking and sat in a wheel chair for months and months, our legs would no longer carry us – this is what happens to the elderly when they give up exercising their muscles. In the same way, we must exercise our faith so that it gets stronger and increases.

Note From Author – We do this by putting on the whole armor. All pieces work together not apart. Our helmet must be on that our mind is protected; our breastplate must be on so that we protect our heart. This all works together in order to face the enemy just like Jesus did in the desert. Our victory will be with our words as well as our actions. The children of Israel were defeated for 40 years because they murmured and complained about their circumstances. We should learn from this and count it all joy for every test we walk through, as discussed, by putting our helmet on to guard our words that what we speak is faith.

2 Corinthians 10:15 (AMP) ¹⁵We do not boast therefore, beyond our proper limit, over other men's labors, but we have the hope and confident expectation that as your faith continues to grow, our field among you may be greatly enlarged, still within the limits of our commission,

This is talking about your individual ministry. If you read all of 2 Corinthians 10, you will see that Paul had been ministering to the Corinthians through letters and on occasions he came face to face with them to share the message given by the Holy Spirit. We must remember, the ministries of man did not begin until the day of Pentecost when the Holy Spirit came upon them. Today, our ministry and our armor is not intact if we are going forth in ourselves. We can do all things through Jesus Christ but outside of Him, we can do nothing. Paul's letters as he proclaimed were bold but face to face, that was not always the case. In this passage of Scripture, it is a pep-talk in order that we engage in the war spiritually and not in the wars of our flesh. We gain greater faith by being prepared spiritually and then going forth where we are called to go and not past those boundaries. The purpose of growing disciples was to meet all ends of the earth and proclaim Jesus Christ.

2 Corinthians 10:3-4 (NIV) ³ For though we live in the world, we do not wage war as the world does. ⁴ The weapons we fight with are not the weapons of the world. On the contrary, they have divine power to demolish strongholds.

Our weapons, our armor was made to fight spiritual battles and not to engage in battles as this world does. This world is defeated, and we too shall be defeated until we learn to not be conformed to this world. We need to go forth growing in faith and the greater things that God has in store for those that seek first His Kingdom

Spiritual Warfare for Kids Beginners II
LESSON 4

ALL AGES TOGETHER – Visual of Roman Armor *(two sets for each group)*

Today Sword of Spirit – Visual

Ephesians 6:10-17 (ESV)
The Whole Armor of God
[10]Finally, be strong in the Lord and in the strength of his might. [11] Put on the whole armor of God, that you may be able to stand against the schemes of the devil. **[12]For we do not wrestle against flesh and blood, but against the rulers, against the authorities, against the cosmic powers over this present darkness, against the spiritual forces of evil in the heavenly places. [13]Therefore take up the whole armor of God, that you may be able to withstand in the evil day, and having done all, to stand firm.** [14]Stand therefore, having fastened on the belt of truth, and having put on the breastplate of righteousness, [15]and, as shoes for your feet, having put on the readiness given by the gospel of peace. **[16]In all circumstances take up the** shield of faith, with which you can extinguish all the flaming darts of the evil one; [17]and take the helmet of salvation, and the **sword of the Spirit, which is the word of God,**

Pray to equip armor brief

(Divide Groups)

(Words to Song will be posted on wall)

Younger kids/Older kids

Will go over lyrics to the fourth chorus of song.
(This is without music – end of lesson will be music)

Verse Four of Song
SATAN ATTACKS BUT HE'S HELL BOUND
WITH MY SWORD OF THE SPIRIT I WILL BRING HIM DOWN
GOT GOD ON MY SIDE AND I CAN'T LOSE
STOMPIN THE DEVIL WITH MY GOSPEL SHOES
** WE WILL WE WILL STOMP YOU (3 TIMES

Review gospel shoes and shield of faith

Open discussion on sword of the Spirit

- What is the Sword of the Spirit?
    - What does the sword protect? *(Pick one child each group to come forward and hold the sword and also have a small sword – and explain that the Roman sword in biblical days at one time was a long sword but later was made into a small sword which became more powerful. A small sword was used in a way for the soldier to get closer to their opponent. The opponent with the long sword was useless if a Roman soldier became too close. The smaller sword proved to be more effective on the battlefield. A soldier learned that standing firmly fixed in one place had great advantage over their enemy instead of trying to cover the whole battlefield. Explain how sword is our offensive weapon)*
- What is this weapon used for? *(Three areas we battle)*

ALL AGES TOGETHER

Song – work on and dance steps *(20 minutes)* – send home with all children the Parent Review for Lesson 4.

PARENTS
(Detailed)
Spiritual Warfare for Kids Beginners II
LESSON 4 REVIEW

Verse Four of Song
SATAN ATTACKS BUT HE'S HELL BOUND
WITH MY SWORD OF THE SPIRIT I WILL BRING HIM DOWN
GOT GOD ON MY SIDE AND I CAN'T LOSE
STOMPIN THE DEVIL WITH MY GOSPEL SHOES
** WE WILL WE WILL STOMP YOU (3 TIMES)

Ephesians 6:10-17 (ESV)
The Whole Armor of God
   ^{10}Finally, be strong in the Lord and in the strength of his might. ^{11} Put on the whole armor of God, that you may be able to stand against the schemes of the devil. **^{12}For we do not wrestle against flesh and blood, but against the rulers, against the authorities, against the cosmic powers over this present darkness, against the spiritual forces of evil in the heavenly places. ^{13}Therefore take up the whole armor of God, that you may be able to withstand in the evil day, and having done all, to stand firm.** ^{14}Stand therefore, having fastened on the belt of truth, and having put on the breastplate of righteousness, ^{15}and, as shoes for your feet, having put on the readiness given by the gospel of peace. **^{16}In all circumstances take up the** shield of faith, with which you can extinguish all the flaming darts of the evil one; ^{17}and take the helmet of salvation, and the **sword of the Spirit, which is the word of God,**

SUMMARY – SWORD OF SPIRIT

What is the Sword of the Spirit?

Main Focus – Your Sword of the Spirit is the Word of God.

Impartation – To win a spiritual war, we use spiritual tools. Natural weapons only work on that which is natural. Your child is learning that those things we cannot see mold the world around us and can change circumstances either in a good way or a bad way dependent on how well they have been trained to fight this war spiritually.

Note From Author – We have learned that the Belt of Truth is the Word of God and now we are learning that the Sword is actually using that which has been stored deep inside of us by God's Word. We must know God intimately through time spent studying to show ourselves approved. Once that is complete where we are grounded in the Word, we are sent forth into the battlefield to gain wisdom as we have discussed. The first tool we pick up in the battlefield is the Shield of Faith in order that we can prevent the fiery darts from penetrating through us. In the battlefield, we face fierce storms in order that the Holy Spirit can remove those areas which weaken us and strengthen those areas which were God-given so that we can fight effectively to gain ground for Jesus Christ. When we look at John the Baptist, we see that he gave his life as a sacrifice to prepare for the first coming of Jesus Christ. Our lives today, as the church, are to be presented as a sacrifice to Our Lord and Savior in order that we gain ground and win souls to prepare for the second-coming of Jesus Christ. As we become effective warriors, our battles will continue, but we will see victory and gain much ground. A soldier learns to use his weapons effectively as he spends time in the battle. You cannot learn to shoot a gun effectively without training. Training means that you practice in order to be effective. Our practice will be in the battlefield, but it will not happen unless we pick up our sword. Our sword becomes effective due to all the time spent studying God's Word combined with all the battles we have been through and gained experience on how to walk through those areas and come out on the other side bringing with us the spoils of our enemy.

We can learn much about spiritual battle when we study the examples given to us in the Old Testament. In 2 Chronicles, there are a few things we need to see.

2 Chronicles 20:15-17 (ESV) [15] And he said, "Listen, all Judah and inhabitants of Jerusalem and King Jehoshaphat: Thus says the LORD to you, 'Do not be afraid and do not be dismayed at this great horde, for <u>the battle is not yours but God's.</u> [16] Tomorrow go down against them. Behold, they will come up by the ascent of Ziz. You will find them at the end of the valley, east of the wilderness of Jeruel. [17] <u>You will not need to fight in this battle. Stand firm,</u>

hold your position, and see the salvation of the L<small>ORD</small> *on your behalf, O Judah and Jerusalem.' Do not be afraid and do not be dismayed. Tomorrow go out against them, and the* L<small>ORD</small> *will be with you."*

First, we need to recognize that as long as our relationship with God is in right standing and we are listening to His voice, our battles will NOT be our own! God goes before us and we follow trusting in Him alone which shows our faith! The other items underlined in verse 17, shows us that God does expect action on our part. He expects us to fight; however, remember, it is a spiritual battle and we fight with spiritual weapons, but we DO NOT just sit on the sidelines crying out to God or crying out to others because we don't know what to do. These Scriptures will show you what to do. We GO – we go out against them (demonic forces) knowing that the Lord will be with us. Now, this may mean that we go by taking action against our specific circumstances but in doing this, it takes our Spiritual Sword which is the Word of God! No battle will ever be won with your own thinking or that of friends. Your thoughts must line up with God's Word.

2 Chronicles 20:20-23 (ESV) [20] And they rose early in the morning and went out into the wilderness of Tekoa. And when they went out, Jehoshaphat stood and said, "Hear me, Judah and inhabitants of Jerusalem! Believe in the L<small>ORD</small> *your God, and you will be established; believe his prophets, and you will succeed." [21] And when he had taken counsel with the people, he appointed those* *who were to sing to the LORD and praise him in holy attire, as they went before the army, and say, "Give thanks to the LORD, for his steadfast love endures forever." ²² And when they began to sing and praise, the LORD set an ambush against the men of Ammon, Moab, and Mount Seir, who had come against Judah, so that they were routed. ²³ For the men of Ammon and Moab rose against the inhabitants of Mount Seir, devoting them to destruction, and when they had made an end of the inhabitants of Seir, they all helped to destroy one another.*

In these passages, we first see that it takes faith. Faith is believing that which has not happened yet. They believed that God was with them and would go before them. They also listened and believed His prophets. Today, what you are listening to better line up with what the prophets in biblical days foretold. However, when we trust and listen, we will succeed in winning our battles. Their particular battle was won by "GOING FORTH" and then by worshiping and praising God. In your spiritual battles, the enemy does not like to hear our voices raise to the heavens glorifying the One that sits on the throne. When we are operating in fear instead of faith, begin worshiping and glorifying Our God and watch the fear subside. All said and done, those that came to bring destruction to God's people destroyed one another.

2 Chronicles 20:25 (ESV) ²⁵ When Jehoshaphat and his people came to take their spoil, they found among them, in great numbers, goods, clothing, and precious things, which they took for *themselves until they could carry no more. They were three days in taking the spoil, it was so much.*

What exactly are our spoils of war? God many times gave them the spoils of war and there were times that He told them to destroy everything including the spoils. However, the spoils in a spiritual battle basically mean that we take back. Your child is learning how to take back those areas which the enemy has taken from them and those they love. The spoils of war are anything that has worth and was in the possession of the enemy. Perhaps, the spoils are merely your joy and peace that the enemy has stolen from you over the years, or the spoils may be fighting to release those you love that are held in bondage. Whatever you may be fighting for, in the battle, your child is learning that God has given us all the fruits of the spirit and these fruits are theirs to keep. Our enemy desires to hold us captive so that we do not flourish in those gifts.

Galatians 5:22-23 (ESV) ²² But the fruit of the Spirit is love, joy, peace, patience, kindness, goodness, faithfulness, ²³ gentleness, self-control; against such things there is no law.

John 10:10 (AMP) ¹⁰The thief comes only in order to steal and kill and destroy. I came that they may have and enjoy life, and have it in abundance (to the full, till it overflows).

In biblical days, the Roman sword was a very long sword but later on, it was made to be much smaller in order to be able to get closer to the enemy which became much more effective. Soldiers learned that they did not have to run all over the battlefield trying to kill as many men as possible. With the smaller sword, they were able to stand their ground in one place and bring down the enemy. The enemy's long sword became useless when they found a Roman soldier too close and they were defeated. In Ephesians, it tells us to stand firm. Fighting in God's army, we have already won, but as long as we are in these bodies, we must remain in active duty and continue saving souls that are lost. As God sends those across our path or as we go where He sends us, we remain standing firmly fixed on the Word of God where we are not moved and we use our spiritual weapon at all times.

What does the sword protect?

Main Focus – The Sword being the Word of God is used to protect God's chosen in all aspects in order that we are able to carry out the plans already set into motion by Our Creator.

Impartation – If you consider yourself a Disciple of Jesus Christ, then you have decided to follow Him. In following Jesus, we lay our lives at the cross and pick up our armor to go forth and do what we were called to do. In doing so, He tells us that not only will signs follow us, but nothing will harm us, nothing we drink shall poison us, etc.

Mark 16:15-18 (ESV) ¹⁵ And he said to them, "Go into all the world and proclaim the gospel to the whole creation. ¹⁶ Whoever believes and is baptized will be saved, but whoever does not believe will be condemned. ¹⁷ And these signs will accompany those who believe: in my name they will cast out demons; they will speak in new tongues; ¹⁸ they will pick up serpents with their hands; and if they drink any deadly poison, it will not hurt them; they will lay their hands on the sick, and they will recover."

If you are chosen, your armor will protect you as you fulfill that which you were called to do.

Note From Author – Of course, we understand that we will still face battles because we are in a spiritual war. However, we will come through on the other side and we all know where this story ends. The Sword can be an offensive or defensive weapon dependent on how it is used. Any weapon can be either but the Shield of Faith is just predominately a defensive weapon. When a weapon is used to protect, that means it defends so it would be a defensive weapon. When a weapon is used to go forth and destroy or bring harm, it becomes an offensive weapon. This is why first in the battlefield, we learn to use the shield in order to protect. As we stand firmly fixed with our shield up, we are proclaiming, *"I am awake with my lamp full Lord, so that my enemy cannot steal, kill or destroy my life or those lives you have entrusted me with!"* When we lift our sword, we are proclaiming, *"Lord, I am ready to go forth into this battle and take back all including the spoils due to war!"*

Daily, our enemy is destroying lives that were meant to serve God. He is destroying people we know and those we love dearly. In biblical days, God's people many times went forth into war led by God to destroy that which was evil. There is evil all around us today as satan and all his demonic forces are using strategies and tactics in order to keep the eyes blinded by the multitudes. Many of those today which are bound by lies, are God's chosen. As warriors, we are called to go forth in order that chains can be broken and lives set free.

Psalm 144:1 (NLV) 144 *Praise and thanks be to the Lord, my rock. He makes my hands ready for war, and my fingers for battle.*

As we understand that we are all called by God and chosen as we become faithful in serving Him, our armor was designed to carry us through the toughest storms and battles in order that we have victory. Victory is going into the war, facing the adversary, coming out on the other side unharmed. Victory is also saving lives of those lost and bound by lies. We are protected when we keep our eyes fixed on the One that has called us into the battle.

What is this weapon, the sword, used for?

Main Focus – Your spiritual sword is used to transform your own life within, the lives of others and to stand against the tactics of the enemy.

Impartation – Our sword is used for the battlefield. Any person that has ever gone into battle in a natural war did so knowing that they might not have come back alive. They accepted their fate, and gave it all they had in order that others would benefit from their sacrifice. This is the great thing about America. Those before us gave their lives in order that our country could be one that was free. We too must give our lives in order that those after us can also be free because with freedom, there is always an enemy striving to take that freedom away. The walk with Jesus is not a self-centered walk but a selfless walk.

Note From Author – There are 3 areas that your child is learning. The Sword of the Spirit which is the Word of God is described as a two-edged sword that will pierce the soul and spirit, joints and marrow, and discern the thoughts and intentions of the heart.

Hebrews 4:12 (ESV) [12]For the word of God is living and active, sharper than any two-edged sword, piercing to the division of soul and of spirit, of joints and of marrow, and discerning the thoughts and intentions of the heart.

We must understand that we cannot deceive God. He knows our hearts. He knows our thoughts and intentions. Serving God and becoming a warrior is an honor but with honor comes examining our own thoughts, motives, intentions, etc. This is the last tool we will pick up in battle, and by the time we get to this place, we must be at a place of total surrender to God. A soldier going into the battlefield can only be a hero based on what is in his own heart. If a soldier is not completely sold out for the cause, he will not give it his whole heart. If we say we are sold out but in our heart there is some reservation, when we face the enemy, he too knows that we are not completely sold out. It takes our heart being in the condition of willingness to let go of everything, lose everything if it must be, and the willingness to die for the cause if it be the Father's will. This is harsh but truth. If we truly desire to save our families from the enemy and take back the spoils that have been stolen from us, such as our joy and peace, it will take a hero that is willing to go the extra mile and throw themselves into the face of the adversary to either do or die.

Before breaking this down into the 3 areas that we battle, let us look at the spoils of war. In biblical days, many times God told His people to take all the spoils once they conquered ground. God desires that our life is full. Jesus came to give us life and to give it in abundance. (John 10:10)

Abundance does not mean material possessions unless those possessions are needed to gain more ground and conquer more territory. Here are two different scenarios – you pick which life you would choose. The first life is filled with riches of this world – good job, good education, big home, fancy cars, money in the bank, exotic vacations, spouse and children, etc. In this family, all seems good. You are in church, your children seem to be great, maybe your relationships all seem good but your relationship with God seems a bit distant. Your life in this scene is filled with raising your children, working to make a good living and have the better things in this life. The second life is filled with the riches of heaven – great relationship with God the Father, Jesus Christ and the Holy Spirit. Daily, you seek the Lord as He leads you to a life of service and giving. Your life is filled with sharing Jesus with others. Your life has become a sacrifice where your plans are made based on the calling that God has placed upon your heart, but your calling has nothing to do with advancing in this world but rather, preparing for the second coming of Jesus Christ. You choose to use your extra resources that God has blessed you with in order to be a light in this dark world. You choose to use your extra time to be the one that says, *"God, send me for I will go."* In all you do and through all your storms, you understand as you call upon the One that has given you breath, He will also be the One that carries you through and calms the storms. He will be the One that shares the secrets of His Word and the yearning of His heart.

In case you did not get this, the first life put all else before Jesus Christ. They put their family and children, their education and job, there advancement into this world to include having the better things that this world has to offer and then after all this was said and done, they went to church. Jesus tells us if anyone loves his mother or father more than me, they are not worthy of heaven.

Matthew 10:34-39 (ESV) [34] "Do not think that I have come to bring peace to the earth. I have not come to bring peace, but a sword. [35] For I have come to set a man against his father, and a daughter against her mother, and a daughter-in-law against her mother-in-law. [36] And a person's enemies will be those of his own household. [37] Whoever loves father or mother more than me is not worthy of me, and whoever loves son or daughter more than me is not worthy of me. [38] And whoever does not take his cross and follow me is not worthy of me. [39] Whoever finds his life will lose it, and whoever loses his life for my sake will find it."

If you have ever wondered how we possibly can love someone that we cannot see more than those that we can see, the way is through our actions. The second life, the calling that God had placed upon their lives became their motivation. In this life, it was filled with service to Our Lord. This life can also have a spouse and children, but their priorities will still be to serve first. Yes, our families come first but not before God. Many times, He calls us to serve others so that He can do a work in the life of those we love. If your family life is a mess, it may be that you need to use your Sword of the Spirit to clean up your own heart first so that you can hear God's voice. Many times God will lead us to service outside of our own home and in doing so, it transforms that within. It begins with our heart and relationship with God first before our other relationships will come together. In this second life, they chose to give everything to God first which is a selfless life. When we choose this kind of life, we actually teach our children that life begins with God first. We teach our children to store treasures in heaven and not on this earth.

I am not implying here that you cannot have the riches of this world and serve God, but what I am implying is that many times those riches of this world distract us from what our true purpose really is on this earth. As disciples, we are to be the "*John the Baptist's"* crying out in the wilderness as we prepare ourselves and others for the second coming of Jesus Christ. Whatever your gifts and whatever your calling may be, as part of the body of Christ, we all work together for His purpose not our own agenda. However, the many today are not stepping up to the platform and giving all they have with their whole heart. The riches of this world can conform us to be more like this world; therefore, our heart should cry out to God saying, *"God, you know me better than I know myself, do not give me the riches of this world if they will transform me to this world and separate my life from You!"* The actual definition of conform means complying with rules and laws which we should, unless they contradict with the Word of God. It also means to be similar to and to agree. If we are trying to be like others in this world, which are not living a Christian life, we are conforming to this world. If we are in agreement with others whose thoughts and actions do not line up with the Word of God, we are in disagreement with the Holy Spirit. Unity with God is being ONE with the Trinity! This is united in thoughts and actions.

Romans 12:2 (ESV) ^{2}Do not be conformed to this world, but be transformed by the renewal of your mind, that by testing you may discern what is the will of God, what is good and acceptable and perfect.

Therefore, when we look at the spoils of war, we need to look at that through the eyes of God in order that the spoils we desire to take back from our enemy will be those that glorify God the Father not bring glory to our self-centered world which on the outsides sends a message that our life is all about material possessions.

This takes us to the first area in which the sword should be used, self.

Luke 2:35 (HCSB) ³⁵and a sword will pierce your own soul—that the thoughts of many hearts may be revealed."

The most important thing the sword will be used for is to transform our own heart. This is the battle within. Before we can be totally sold out, we must be transformed in our minds and thoughts that our agenda becomes His will. The sword being the Word of God comes to life at this point where it is not just knowledge but it becomes our wisdom. At this place, in our storms, we come to know God's heart intimately where we understand His intentions and calling upon our own lives. The puzzle begins to make sense and our purpose in this life is made known. However, it is at this place where we choose to either remain connected with this world or we let go to find the greater treasures in this life. Moses understood that the greater treasures were so much more than the riches of this world. There are no greater treasures than the assurance that Our God is madly in love with each of us. There are no greater treasures than knowing, as His children, he desires for us to share in those riches which cannot be seen because they are there for those that love Him.

As stated above, we are to be ONE with the trinity. Jesus prayed to the Father that we all be ONE with them.

John 17:20-23 (ESV) [20] "I do not ask for these only, but also for those who will believe in me through their word, [21] that they may all be one, just as you, Father, are in me, and I in you, that they also may be in us, so that the world may believe that you have sent me. [22] The glory that you have given me I have given to them, that they may be one even as we are one, [23] I in them and you in me, that they may become perfectly one, so that the world may know that you sent me and loved them even as you loved me."

This is an example of who we should be. There is God the Father, God the Son and God the Holy Spirit. They are 3 but they are One together because they are in unity. When a man and woman get married, they become ONE. They are 2 people but ONE together because they should be in unity together. Unity means that we have the same agenda. We have the same goals in mind. We agree together and when we are not in agreement, that is where the Word of God comes into play. In a marriage, there should be 3, the husband, wife, and

Jesus Christ. If Jesus was the center of marriages today, we would not see divorce. Jesus being the center of our thoughts means that when there is conflict, it does not matter what we think because what He thinks over rules our thoughts. This takes being humble and not trying to control your relationships because control is not being in unity. Jesus should be the head over the family unit today. So, in order to have this relationship with Jesus as head, takes us submitting to the Holy Spirit as He uses the sword to take all that is not God out of our heart and fill it with the love of God. Love is the greatest and with love, we will be in unity with God the Father, God the Son and God the Holy Spirit as Jesus prayed, *"Father, let them be ONE with us!"*

The next battle coincides with the first battle, the battle in this world or the battle without. Once our mind begins to be renewed to the mind of Jesus Christ, our desires will begin to change but the battle is not over just yet. satan will come on the scene and remain on the scene during this storm due to fear that you may actually cross over and become that disciple that will chose to let go of this world. To clarify, the battle within begins to shape our heart to be united with Jesus Christ. We come to the place where our heart actually breaks for those things which grieve Our Father, but the battle has just begun to heat up, and the next phase will be stepping into the furnace. The battle in this world is where we actually begin to let go of one thing at a time. That is why I refer to it as the battle without. Going through this stage myself, I remember for 6 months fighting my own desires and my own will and my own agenda. I remember making choices to let go of things I once thought were so important. I remember making choices to do things I would have never done and making other choices not to do things that I would never have stopped doing. This is the battle without. It is learning to do without things that actually keep us from developing that intimate relationship with the Father in order that we hear His voice and submit to that voice. However, it is at this place where God radically begins to work on behalf of our life. If you are willing to serve the God of the Universe and sell out to His cause, He will radically take hold of your life.

1 Peter 5:7 (AMP) ⁷Casting the whole of your care [all your anxieties, all your worries, all your concerns, once and for all] on Him, for He cares for you affectionately and cares about you watchfully.

Matthew 6:33 (AMP) ³³But seek (aim at and strive after) first of all His kingdom and His righteousness (His way of doing and being right), and then all these things taken together will be given you besides.

Most people run to church when they are faced with a crisis, but what they fail to see is that God is saying, *"Seek Me first... seek Me first...,"* and it is then that all things will be given to you. We can cast all our cares upon Him because He does care for us, but first we must seek Him. First, we must come to know Him. First, we must learn every aspect about our armor so that when we come to Him, we will know Him. So, when we come to Him, we understand that it has everything to do with allowing that Sword to pierce our own heart in order that we are in unity as One with Him.

*Psalm 138:8 (NKJV) ⁸ The L*ORD *will perfect that which concerns me; Your mercy, O L*ORD*, endures forever; Do not forsake the works of Your hands.*

Once we come to understand the first two areas that the Sword is used for, the last place we use our Sword is the battle with the enemy. We should never go forth to battle satan without being fully equipped and fully knowledgeable. We see far too often, Christians get a taste of spiritual warfare and begin going forth swinging their sword with all other parts of the armor not intact. Imagine a battle in the natural where men and women went to boot camp and were only taught how to use a gun. They were then shipped off to the battlefield and dropped off on enemy terrain in a country that they knew nothing about and had no guidance on the tactics or strategies of the enemy they would be fighting. Get this picture in your head. They are in a field shooting their gun in all directions as the enemy is surrounded about them. They are turning in circles shooting in all different directions because they are overwhelmed and have no clue what is going on. They are probably screaming and shouting but that is doing them no good. How long do you think they would last in that scenario?

We cannot win the battles in enemy territory without being fully engaged. We would never send men and women into the battlefield in a natural war if they had not first completed a boot camp designed to train them in all areas. We want our troops to be fully equipped with all they would need to bring the enemy down in a natural war. We want our troops to gain ground and take back what has been taken because this is the purpose of war. We go forth with a purpose or we don't go forth. You would not want to ask a soldier why they were fighting and receive the answer, *"I don't know!"* I know there have been wars in this world that didn't make sense but fighting in God's army should always make sense. The battle going forth will be after you have gained the knowledge and wisdom needed to conquer and then it will take place in enemy terrain. We don't have to wait for the enemy to come after us, we can go forth as Christians to do damage in the spiritual realm or in the heavenly realm on enemy terrain, knowing that Jesus gave us power and authority over ALL and that nothing can destroy us or bring us down.

Luke 10:19 (AMP) [19]Behold! I have given you authority and power to trample upon serpents and scorpions, and [physical and mental strength and ability] over all the power that the enemy [possesses]; and nothing shall in any way harm you.

Without your Sword of the Spirit, you will never be able to destroy enemy forces that have targeted you and your family. Your sword only becomes an offensive weapon when you go to battle ready to take back what has been taken from you and those you are praying for. When we go forth, we do so to destroy those forces set up against us. We go forth into enemy terrain to fight for what is rightfully ours. Being a warrior is not about sitting on the sidelines as I have said. Soldiers today are not trained and then sent back home to do nothing. We do not become warriors in order that we can just go back to civilian life and live as the rest of this world. Jesus tells us to always be on guard. He tells us to stay awake. We are in a spiritual war today, and we must be watching and preparing now.

Luke 21:8-17 (NKJV) [8]And He said: "Take heed that you not be deceived. For many will come in My name, saying, 'I am He,' and,

'The time has drawn near.' Therefore do not go after them. ⁹ But when you hear of wars and commotions, do not be terrified; for these things must come to pass first, but the end will not come immediately." ¹⁰ Then He said to them, "Nation will rise against nation, and kingdom against kingdom. ¹¹ And there will be great earthquakes in various places, and famines and pestilences; and there will be fearful sights and great signs from heaven. ¹² But before all these things, they will lay their hands on you and persecute you, delivering you up to the synagogues and prisons. You will be brought before kings and rulers for My name's sake. ¹³ But it will turn out for you as an occasion for testimony. ¹⁴ Therefore settle it in your hearts not to meditate beforehand on what you will answer; ¹⁵ for I will give you a mouth and wisdom which all your adversaries will not be able to contradict or resist. ¹⁶ You will be betrayed even by parents and brothers, relatives and friends; and they will put some of you to death. ¹⁷ And you will be hated by all for My name's sake."

1 Peter 5:8 (NKJV) ⁸Be sober, be vigilant; because your adversary the devil walks about like a roaring lion, seeking whom he may devour.

In fact, he is destroying those today that have failed to love the truth! When we fail to love the truth, we venture into territories where we become prey. Think about a real lion in the jungle. They roam to and fro seeking their prey, but what are they seeking for? Animals that are weaker become prey for the lion. The young and the weak become their prey, but those animals that venture off alone and leave the herd also become prey.

1 Corinthians 16:13(NKJV) ¹³ Watch, stand fast in the faith, be brave, be strong.

Our enemy is roaming to destroy those that have no desires to learn of God. He is roaming to destroy those that are too busy to take time out to become a warrior in God's Army. He is roaming to destroy those that do not spend time to ask, seek and knock. When we do not study the Word of God, we are weak spiritually and become that weak prey for the lion, for satan. When we stray away from the flock, we are targeted by satan, and demons come in with temptations so that we fall away. This is why we are told in Hebrews not to forsake coming together with other Christians. We cannot go this road alone.

Hebrews 10:24-25 (ESV) ²⁴ And let us consider how to stir up one another to love and good works, ²⁵ not neglecting to meet together, as is the habit of some, but encouraging one another, and all the more as you see the Day drawing near.

The purpose in biblical days of meeting together was all about stirring each other up. This should not fall upon one person but all Christians. We grow and we become witnesses of our faith continually sharing the Good News of all God has done in our lives and is doing in our lives. Today, when we step into church, the multitudes are broken, hurting people. The sad part is that the majority remain in that state because there are not enough warriors going forth battling for the saints. We have a Sword and it is to be used once we gain insight. We should be striving to grow so that God can use us mightily.

We are told in Thessalonians why the many do not travel the same road as the first disciples.

2 Thessalonians 2:9-10 (ESV) ⁹ The coming of the lawless one is by the activity of Satan with all power and false signs and wonders, ¹⁰ and with all wicked deception for those who are perishing, because they refused to love the truth and so be saved.

We have refused to love the truth and therefore, be saved. This is the key to a life following Jesus Christ. The Truth is the Word of God. Outside of His Word there is no truth. Any argument or conflict can be judged only by the Word of God. It does not matter what this world says, what the many different denominations say, what your family says, teachers, friends, etc. If there is disagreement, it can be settled by God's Word. In the beginning was the Word and all we see was made by the Word. This is not the actual bible which we pick up, that is merely paper but it is what is written in the bible. God's words are powerful. The Word always was and the Word became flesh and dwelt among us. When we have refused to love the Truth, we have refused to love Jesus Christ. If a man says he loves God but hates his brother, the Word says he is a liar. How then can we love God? The key is in 2 Thessalonians. The Word is the Truth. We cannot fall in love with Jesus Christ without the Word of God in us because that is Jesus. To know Jesus is to know the written Word of God. It is who He is. When people say they struggle with reading the Word or when Christians say they seldom have time to read the Word of God, they are not in love with Truth. How then can we be in love with Truth? If you struggle to read and study the Truth, this is where you cry out by asking and seeking. Those that do not read and study God's Word will never have a love for the Truth until they seek for it diligently. We pick up the Word daily and we ask,

"Lord, open up the Scriptures that they come alive in my life!" The Word is living and is life to those that find it. We continually seek where we dig deep into His Word, the Truth for answers to our own lives and we again, ask, *"Lord, show me the answers and give me insight. Father, open my eyes that they see and my ears that they hear!"* Jesus said seek and you will find, knock and the door will open. Yes, you will find and yes, the door will open but only for those that diligently seek Him.

2 Thessalonians 2:11-12 (ESV). [11] Therefore God sends them a strong delusion, so that they may believe what is false, [12] in order that all may be condemned who did not believe the truth but had pleasure in unrighteousness.

It continues where those that failed to love the Truth will believe that which is false. God will allow you to be condemned and destroyed. He has given us His Word; He gave us Jesus. Everything has been done for us to receive salvation and eternal life with the Father, but it takes warriors that are willing to go to the next level of Christianity by giving up their own life and living a life for Jesus Christ.

One more time, we need to get this deep within. We fail to see that Jesus is Truth. In the beginning was the Word and there was nothing without the Word because the Word made all. Jesus was the Word made flesh. Jesus is the light of this world and without Him there was nothing and there will be nothing. Jesus is the way, the TRUTH, and the life. Without Jesus, we have nothing. Without Jesus, our lives are meaningless. Without Him we can do nothing but with Him all things can be accomplished according to the will of the Father. If you find yourself in a place where you seldom read the Word of God or you seldom have a desire to seek Scriptures, it is time to cry out to God to put those desires and hunger within so that you have NOT failed to love the TRUTH! Without the love for truth within, we will be given over to believe that which is false.

To be fully engaged in God's Army takes enlisting in Boot Camp. In Boot Camp there is much training to prepare Warriors for God's Army. In Boot Camp, you will become filled with the Holy Spirit which will teach you all things and make the Scriptures come alive for you. The disciples in the New Testament would not have done all the things they did after Jesus left them if it had not been for the filling of the Holy Spirit. Without the Holy Spirit, our armor will not be intact. Without the Holy Spirit, the Scriptures will not come alive to us. Without the Holy Spirit, we will not be able to do ALL things through Jesus Christ because it is the Holy Spirit that brings us to be ONE with them!

John 16:7-15 (ESV) [7] Nevertheless, I tell you the truth: it is to your advantage that I go away, for if I do not go away, the Helper will not come to you. But if I go, I will send him to you. [8] And when he comes, he will convict the world concerning sin and righteousness and judgment: [9] concerning sin, because they do not believe in me;

[10]concerning righteousness, because I go to the Father, and you will see me no longer; [11]concerning judgment, because the ruler of this world is judged. [12]"I still have many things to say to you, but you cannot bear them now. [13]When the Spirit of truth comes, he will guide you into all the truth, for he will not speak on his own authority, but whatever he hears he will speak, and he will declare to you the things that are to come. [14]He will glorify me, for he will take what is mine and declare it to you. [15]All that the Father has is mine; therefore I said that he will take what is mine and declare it to you."

When the Scriptures come alive to you, there will be a love for TRUTH! You will know that love is in you because your desire will be to continually seek to greater depths to know the Father, Son and Holy Spirit.

"Lord, I desire that the Sword of the Spirit pierce through my own heart in order to show me what is truth and what is not. I desire that my heart be broken in order that I come to know who You are in all truth. Break my heart Lord for what breaks yours and let my desires be for those things that you desire."

CONCLUSION BY THE AUTHOR

This book is only a guide to help those that desire to be in a more intimate relationship with Our Creator. Being a Warrior in God's Army begins in the home with those in spiritual authority over that home. Our children are molded according to our ways and our character. The good news is that our character can be re-shaped into the character of Jesus Christ no matter what age. There is so much more to learn about spiritual warfare and my hopes are that this book will be the beginning for a life long journey into the knowledge, wisdom and understanding of Our Heavenly Father.

For more reading and understanding on Spiritual Warfare, the author's full-version of Spiritual Warfare will be released fall of 2015. Look for the title, *Sustaining in Battle… Breaking Through the Storm*, by Jolene McCall.

References

Introduction

1. 10 natural disasters that changed the world by Victoria Bischoff on Mar 16, 2011 at 15:48 http://citywire.co.uk/money/10-natural-disasters-that-changed-the-world/a479056#i=4
2. Love Worth Finding Ministries with Adrian Rogers, *Beware the Kidnapper.* http://www.lwf.org/site/PageServer
3. Lauren Daigle – Trust In You (Lyric Video) – YouTube. https://www.youtube.com/watch?v=qv-SXz_exKE

www.ingramcontent.com/pod-product-compliance
Lightning Source LLC
LaVergne TN
LVHW051831080426
835512LV00018B/2812